Dead-End Sex

Printed by CreateSpace,
An Amazon.com Company

PDC Books,
POB 138, Yehud 56275
Israel
www.pdc-psyche.net

WGA W registry:1839072
US C/O:1-3365971861

ISBN-13-9781533393012
ISBN-10-153339301X

Dead-End Sex

by

Arnold Holtzman

For all the good people who had made their way to my door and had shared with me the rich and unique facets of their lives. They are the true authors of this book.

CONTENTS
PAGE

Author's note:

Without exception, all of the names appearing in the vignettes offered here are the author's invention. None identify any of the characters described in these stories. Any resemblance, if such exist, is unintended and entirely coincidental.

1. Starting out

He never looks at me while we're doing it," complained Christine. Just as often the complaint would be reversed and it would be Kenny who would be overtaken by a familiar bitterness saying that he would always be there by himself. "I'm inside pumping away," as he put it, "but Christine never looks at me. I'm not even sure she knows I'm there." He described how, with her eyes tightly shut, she would keep her head turned sharply to one side.

"It's been like this as far back as I can remember. The feeling would always be as though I was there by myself – and worse, that she was using me." Kenny confessed, in his silent heart, that he would feel much the same way when he masturbated.

For Christine, the problem was 180° in the other direction. It would be the queasy feeling she would have when Kenny locked himself into her vagina but never into *her*. To her dismay she faulted Kenny for suddenly morphing into a mechanical droid who would pick just that fleeting moment of intimacy to visit a distant planet. Wherever he was, it wasn't with her.

Then it's over. They come apart and attend to their ablution rituals. With conscious effort, perhaps, they succeed in masking their disappointment, but they radiate no joy in the wake of a sudden, hard drop in room temperature.

Given doggie style and another 63 variants, the Kama Sutra may have been written specifically for these libidinally insulated people. However the missionary position remains the only one meant to have the partners experience something akin to the original, magical, bonding with the mother when the two had once merged into a perfect organic oneness. The very same sense of completion, total envelopment and total well-being that the neonate and infant had known, remains in the deepest recesses of its subconscious mind as a vivid and very real reference to itself throughout his or her life. It is a reference that begs repetition. Just as the wild salmon is drawn to return to the waters in which it had spawned, so too would this person be powerfully driven to relive the richness and rewards of this complete bonding with another.

Unfortunately, not always do the partners share the same early history. Inasmuch as her infant may be more precious to the mother than her own life, the actual bonding with the neonate may conceivably have lacked an organic quality. The neonate/infant, even in the embrace of its mother, remained a body apart from her own.

We explore this flawed chemistry at somewhat greater length in the pages ahead, but it would suffice to note that this infant, as an adult, would not have the merging of the two into one as a natural and familiar reference to itself. The critical issue here is that without this reference in the package of a person's real life possibilities, the actual act of a physical union is outside the realm of these possibilities. The experience, when it does happen, almost invariably feels entirely unnatural.

The sexual experience for this couple eventually crashes. One partner, ever overtaken with a sense of emptiness and abandonment, is chronically disappointed. The other, wishing at some subconscious level for the copulation to serve as a corrective experience – corrective in the sense that it might deliver that which was vacant in the original mother experience – knows only the erosive frustration of missing a vital constituent in his or her emotional life.

If this couple happen to be married to each other the problems lead to an eventual divorce. This is because the needs and drives of both will promote predictable, if inconvenient, and wholly incompatible programs. They are at a loss even to communicate in a manner the other side can grasp. One will remain open to a genuine bonding experience with a single partner (even if that single partner is married to another, as often happens). The other will be moved to believe that the next partner

9

will deliver that elusive sense of attachment and completion. Almost invariably however, until the later years of this person's life, there will be no end to this unforgiving search for the treasure possibly buried in the "next" partner.

As the reader will soon find, Kenny and Christine had no monopoly on dead-end sex.

2. The Obsessive-Compulsive

Here we come upon what many popularly describe as compulsive freaks. In the jargon of the professional behavioral specialist this category of disorder includes the somewhat rigid, energetic and single-minded workaholics. They tend to think of themselves as perfectionists. Inasmuch as their teeth invariably remain hidden behind convoluted intellectualizations and rationalizations, they strive for controls with the passion of a determined pit bull unleashed and on steroids.

As often as not the women most attracted to these largely well-meaning gentlemen are the mildly neurotic astronauts who live by their crystals, candles, cats, and carrot juice. Here are the vegans, the Virgos, and the writers of deep, esoteric verses meant to make the world a far better place. Their most pressing problem is that their feet rarely find the ground. Marching for peace and animal rights do not generally contribute to paying their share of the rented flat, and, unfortunately, the tools one can enlist to keep body attached to soul are largely foreign to them. In their hearts they cannot see themselves waitressing through their thirties. They tried their hand at making scented soaps and candles but with a talent falling short even of their marketing skills.

What cheese is to the mouse these men are to these ladies. Here is the engineer with a persona fixed firmly to Mother Earth. His every word seems carved in stone. These people have a sure grip on the reins of their lives and prefer not to be beholden to anyone for anything. They prefer the familiar to the unfamiliar. They understand everything and have answers that would put philosophers to shame. Best of all, they know how to fix a leaky faucet and silence squeaky door hinges.

What these ladies do project is a profound spiritual aura, which, in the minds of the obsessive-compulsives would surely complete their own lives. More than being in the proximity of this free-floating mindset they are convinced they could own it. Along with making it theirs and finding it beautiful they are certain they are worldly and liberal enough to be open to it – absolutely convinced that they understand its every nuance. So what we have here, in essence, is a symbiotic relationship akin to the clownfish finding security in the tentacles of a warm and inviting sea anemone.

The only difficulty here is that the sea anemone's live-and-let-live attitude in this partnership is an entirely unknown component in the land version of this creature. It is only a question of time before he delivers his (soon battle scarred) astronaut lady to the real world. When that happens his fair, angelic and fragile clownfish morphs into a tempestuous ninja warrior monk with swinging nunchucks and sends him, quite unceremoniously, to a distant station outside her life forever. All he gets to leave behind are generous alimony payments.

From the start he lived with the absolute certainty that she was impossibly grateful to have him in her life. He was convinced that no one knew better than she herself did how fortunate she was to find shelter under his benevolent thumb. He would be her mentor ready to guide her unerringly through the vicissitudes of life's byways.

When they first got into bed he was gentle, considerate and accommodated her every whim as though intuitively anticipating them. She might have been the manufacture of the rarest porcelain judging from the softness of his touch and his quiet concern. He was mildly disappointed that she failed to compliment his lovemaking skills or the dimensions of his lusting appendage. It was a disappointment, however, that he was unable to repress for very long. In fact it was voiced in innocent tones the very next time they were in bed together. It was important for him to know whether she had ever experienced better sex than what they were presently having. And did his penis satisfy her?

Of course he couldn't wait until their orgasms were behind them. No. It was vital that he get these critically important statistics at that precise moment. After all, however unlikely, but if adjustments on his part were called for he could still make them.

A bucket of ice water poured over her head would have tempered her mood less and not detached her mind from her body with the severity his words had had done. They ravaged her sensibilities. Gritting her teeth she pushed him away, none too gently, and went for her clothes. Outwardly he tried to deflate her ballooning anger with profuse apologies explaining, with hand on heart, that he wanted only to be sure that everything would, and could, be perfect for her. Inwardly he gave her a double minus and wondered how he might yet go about getting those answers.

He never believed in vacations but when forced he would organize their schedule in the manner of a general preparing for battle. The day would begin at precisely 7:45 with a buffet breakfast. At 9 am they were down for tennis in their spotless and freshly ironed white outfits. At 10.15 a second coffee. 11 to noon was their hour with the personal trainer followed by… She would have much preferred to spend the entire day soaking up the sun at the pool or seashore.

Sex became a rigidly fixed routine. The days and hours were set in concrete as was the act itself. They lived by strict formula. Everything had a beginning, a middle and an end. He would instruct her how to lie, where he wanted to feel her hands, and what he wanted to hear her say. He tried convincing her that her complaints were really rooted in unfinished business from her early childhood, not his fault, and that she should be more appreciative of his efforts to please her.

More than once she felt herself at the edge of insanity. But then she was no longer that naive innocent making her way in a fairytale world. Her skin had thickened, her knuckles had hardened, and she made expert use of those nunchucks. Her husband made his inglorious departure with his tail between his legs. She met an airline pilot, divorced, and with a daughter about her age. He became her lover. The image of herself that would be mirrored in his eyes made surrendering to him so wonderful. The lightness had returned to her chest, and she reveled in the joy and sheer happiness they brought to their trysts.

3. Keeping With This Theme

Sue was Tom's girlfriend for almost a year. She was what some would call an astronaut (yes, I know I'm repeating myself), as she always seemed moved by things ethereal. These would include being carried away emotionally by the simplest flowers and the deepest poets. She herself would dabble with songs and poems that were never delivered anywhere but to the drawers and boxes in her room – all of which were secured with locks. When they broke up it was at her initiative. She said that at first what he gave her was the sense of security and stability, and that with him she could feel herself on firm ground. But she increasingly felt herself choking on the rigid boundaries he set on virtually every aspect of her life, and especially so on their relationship. She accused him of living by fixed "formulas" that he would force upon both of them. "If I needed a preacher in my life," she once screamed at him, "I'd go to a church." Tom would explain that it was his nature to be a perfectionist and that he only wanted the best for both of them. This carried little weight with Sue.

A few years later he met and married Elizabeth. Not long before their marriage he was asked by an associate at his office if he loved her.

Tom's reply was something in this vein. "Liz is absolutely gorgeous. She has a body that might have come from the pages of Playboy. You should see how men look at her. We are both terrific with each other in bed. She can put together a sushi better than anything you'll find on the Ginza. Our parents are both Episcopalian. Her father is the chairman of the board of the XYZ Company and the whole family, Liz included, is swimming in big bucks. She has absolutely everything I am looking for in a woman. So of course I love her."

When Tom turned the same question back to his associate and his own fiancée, what he got by way of reply was, "*Geez*, I don't know why. I just love her."

Their marriage lasted just over a year. Tom complained that Liz was putting on weight in the wrong places. Liz was less specific. She thought he was simply a programmed robot impossible to live with.

4. "It hurts. It just hurts."

I recognized Marcia the moment she entered the office and recalled to the last detail the session we had almost five years earlier. Clutching her hand was a lovely little girl of about three decked out in an immaculate white and blue sailor's suit.

It was mostly about a woman's thing – something that might describe a pocket of autism in an otherwise healthy, balanced and socially active individual. These ladies can be stunningly attractive, well educated, enjoy successful careers, and make friends easily. What they cannot do is tolerate the presence of a penis within their bodies. This was Marcia's story.

The popular name associated with this condition is *vaginismus* and is explained as a strong muscular contraction of the vagina immediately prior to coitus. At some point in what these troubled ladies tended to believe were their diminished lives, they invite the intervention of medical people purported to be experts in the resolution of this problem. Let me say at the outset that these well-meaning doctors, inasmuch as they insist that the problem is 100% treatable and claiming success rates verging on 100%, they haven't the slightest notion what, in fact, they are dealing with. For starters this isn't a medical issue at all, and their programs of intervention

are entirely mechanical – as often as not compounding
the damage by the gross blunting of the patient's natural
libidinal expressions. Psychiatrists distinguish between
acquired and lifelong forms of vaginismus. It would be
more helpful if the medical people also distinguished
between the two.

Vaginismus has more in common with Pavlov's dog
than with anything appearing in medical textbooks, but
more about this later. The point is that the therapist is
not dealing with the actual physical manifestation which
keeps the penis external to the body, but with a
condition wherein the penis, *even having penetrated
with minimal pain*, triggers an acute anxiety reaction.
These aren't just words to grasp analytically. An acute
anxiety reaction can deliver an individual to
experience something very nearly akin to a paralysis
of every organ in the body. Marcia tried to have me
understand that coitus felt entirely unnatural to her,
forcing her to suffer what she described as something
altogether alien and painful in her body. That
appendage simply didn't belong there. To describe
it merely as disturbing was not to understand the feeling
at all. The trauma she had once suffered that came
closest to this experience, she offered, was when she
was nine years old and having an enema forcibly
administered to her by the family doctor.

19

Vaginismus is merely the condition fixed at the far end of the spectrum when measuring the level of pain, anguish – even resentment – associated with the penetration of the penis. The question Marcia put before me, and with which she battled endlessly in her mind was what was an otherwise warm and healthy girl to do if she falls in love, wishes to marry and to bring children into the world?

From the session we were presently having I learned that a soft-spoken and gentle young man came into her life, and a meaningful relationship ensued. There soon came an hour when she understood that she would be wise to share his libidinal drives for an intimate union of their bodies. She cloaked her revulsion and anxiety with smiles and soft words. Her partner translated this as shyness and the modesty that seemed so becoming to those without much experience. In his heart he came to love her even more. Very likely he too lacked much experience because very soon after penetration he would discharge his sperm into a well lubricated condom and exit her body – much to her relief. She would tell him how happy he was making her. After a time they married.

They were in their mid-twenties and to keep from disappointing him she had accommodated his energetic libidinal passions just about every day. However, with the increased familiarity with her body he began increasingly to extend the sex act for what he believed would be for *her* pleasure. Very soon he found himself being repeatedly asked to have his orgasm hardly a moment after having penetrated. She complained of it beginning to feel sore, dry and painful "down there".

The ritual of their coupling in bed was reduced to once a week. Then perhaps once in two weeks. When her suffering had persisted he suggested she visit an appropriate doctor and that she did, only to learn that she was naturally small. Ointments were prescribed along with the suggestion that she lend herself to hot relaxing salt baths. That doctor had also mentioned helpful exercises but these she immediately dismissed from her recollection of her half hour visit which, in her mind, was shameful enough

The pain, tension, gross unpleasantness and general discomfort never left her. But neither would she deny them sleeping together when the thought that his forced celibacy might move him to seek redress in the arms of another partner. Before a year had passed she became pregnant. It mattered less now to her that he might seek a liaison with another woman. In her heart she had long wished to be off sex altogether, and her excuse now would be understandable and graced with legitimacy.

21

It would be fair to note that this lovely and intelligent lady was not born with this condition. It was neither a genetic factor nor otherwise inherited. It was entirely a function of conditioning that was rather more insidious and certainly more damaging than the manner in which Pavlov got his dog to salivate on cue.

Again we have a feature of her early mother-experience that delivered the conditioning responsible for her distress as an adult. At birth the mother had given the child occasional access to her body. Yet for whatever reason the mother could not bring herself to bond neither physically nor emotionally with her daughter. The possible reasons can fill textbooks. The neonate/infant may have found all the natural targets of its innate libidinal needs on the mother's body, *but it had never known the experience of its own body serving as the natural libidinal targets originating with a source beyond itself.*

Which is to say that the absence of this primal experience became indelibly grafted onto the life programs available to Marcia. With this unfortunate history no experience can be more unnatural and unnerving to her, or, indeed, to any woman sharing a like history, then having their bodies serve as the target for the very physical, libidinal drives of others.

The session with Marcia carried on for a full hour. For the most part it was rich with understanding and acceptance. The only jarring moment came when we were both on our feet. I was about to open the door for her when she added, almost as a by-the-way, that she felt blessed having her daughter in her life, but somehow found it impossible to feel any deep motherly attachment to her.

5. Not every explorer is a Columbus

It sometimes crossed Mabel's mind that perhaps there was something of the whorish nymphomaniac in her personality. She was divorced, educated, always fashionably dressed, held a high-paying, responsible position in a national finance company, and could spend virtually every night of the week (more when vacationing) in bed with a different man – an exaggeration, she knew, but not by much. When finding herself without a new partner Mabel would reluctantly return to someone she had previously been with and whose company she may have enjoyed. But in her mind twice would invariably be one time overmuch.

She knew she had her counterpart among men. This lifestyle, after all, was far simpler for a macho persona to accommodate, and risked only a fraction of the consequences a woman would have to be mindful of. Life, the thought, was so unfair in this respect. The man would have his condo a whisker below the stratosphere in his high-rise. Floor to ceiling windows would overlook a huge expanse of the night city. No drug company could offer a more potent aphrodisiac for any lady visiting here for the first time. That, at least had been her experience. His female counterpart would have either the least expensive 2 room arty apartment at the swankiest address, or, what she had – a huge loft with dark hardwood floors, a massive butcher's block in the kitchen/dining room and plumbing accessories, Malibu style, floating in midair. No gentleman visiting here for the first time ever thought she was an ordinary lay.

Truth be told, Mabel didn't much enjoy the sex she was addicted to. The only ecstasy she knew came as a hallucinogenic drug for the high school crowd. Time and again she tried convincing herself that enough was enough. But unless a strep throat, a vaginal discharge, or an innocent STD (innocent in the sense that it was no match for penicillin) gave her pause, the compulsion persisted.

She was paying her shrink five hundred good American dollars for every visit – once each week. After five years what Mabel learned was that as an infant her hysterical mother had never let her explore the world... that everything she got near to might have been breakable, dirty or poison. It was his professional opinion that her mother was also paranoid, but that, to his mind, was small change. And then after keeping Mabel bonded at her breast forever "this fine woman", he insisted, "this perfect mother suddenly disappeared".

"What do you mean "disappeared"? She was always at home.

"Disappeared! Disappeared! Does it sound like I'm talking Chinese to you? If you cried, did she come? If you were hungry, did she come? If you crapped in your diaper, did she show up? "If you wanted to know that she was still there, did she show her face? No! No! No! No! No! That's disappearing! Here, in China or in Timbuktu!"

Mable had started to cry.

"Oh fuck the crying" he suddenly shouted at her, half rising from his massive, rocking, easy char. "And leave a check with me this time. That's two weeks."

The bottom line was that Mabel was still desperately looking for her mother and by screwing like a rabbit with every man she met she imagined that bonding... that physically attaching herself to another body, was her ticket.

"Not every explorer is a Columbus", he had said. "Not everyone finds America."

And *ka-ching... ka-ching... ka-ching* went his cash register, thought Mabel, shaking her head. This bloodsucker sure found America. Nevertheless, she always left his office wondering what she would wear for her next appointment that might have him look at her as a woman.

6. "Where did he put my nipple?"

She was in her late 30's, slim, dark eyes, blue shadow, with black hair pulled tightly back and moussed to her scalp. She had been referred to me by her sister, a clinical social worker and a part time instructor at a dance studio. I knew there was a third, and younger sister in the family, who was quite popular as a fashion model.

There was no preamble.

"I want you to look at my breasts" she said, sitting tight and tense at the very edge of her armchair. The words were spoken in a hurried rush even before I settled myself on my own seat. Almost in disbelief, I couldn't believe I was hearing what I thought I was hearing, I asked her if she wouldn't like a cup of coffee before we began our session. It was our first meeting and I suspected from the nature of that request that it might be our last.

"I want you to look at my breasts" she repeated. "I have to know what you think."

"Well, I can't," I replied hoping she would catch a stern tone in my voice. "If it was permitted I'd think about it. But *a*, it's totally unethical and *b*, it's totally against the law in my profession." Hoping to lighten our terse exchanges I asked her to first give me a chance to learn something about herself.

"And afterwards?"

"Out of the question."

"Aren't you a doctor?"

"Not a medical doctor, but if that's what you thought plainly you were misinformed and we best stop right here."

"I know you are not that kind of a doctor, but Carla (her social worker sister) told me to talk to you before I go to a lawyer and the police.

(The plot suddenly thickened.) "Coffee?" I make a perfect espresso." Carla wasn't her sister's name and my visitor's name wasn't Janet – the name we'll use – but everything else in the account that follows carries the Kosher for Passover label.

Janet had had a number of "serious" boyfriends since high school. What distinguished the serious from the non-serious was that she invariably had sex with the former and mostly cellphone sms's with the latter. She was 14 when she had had her first serious relationship. Her partner at the time was 15 years old and the sex came in the wake of his sincere promise to marry her after he'd finish with school and get a job. Somehow he disappeared without leaving behind a trace as to his whereabouts.

She persevered with her loyalty to him until her 16th birthday when she met a string bean basketball player who gave her great seats at their college league games. She would find herself becoming sexually aroused watching him win applause with each basket he scored knowing that he belonged to her (in a manner). He was also the source of an infection that had obliged to her make her first visit to a gynecologist.

There were several men after him, and with each she would convince herself that their passionate lovemaking would surely to lead to the altar. None carried in that direction, but the last fellow suggested that breast implants would greatly improve her appearance... that she looked fabulous even now, but that her breasts fell kind of flat. He must have thought of himself as being admirably honest when he added that they reminded him of the empty paps he'd seen on native African tribal women on the National Geographic channel.

Janet had always suffered the thought that she was without the spindly flamingo legs and the Modigliani neck that invested her younger sister's life with such bounce, and which promised her nothing less than a marzipan future. But her breasts were not unlike those of her sisters so that this gentleman's rather ungallant observation merely added to everything else she felt was wrong about her body. What else could explain why all the "serious" men in her life found every excuse to leave her. (We will make an effort to come up with an answer in the next account of Janet's reflections on her life.)

I'm not sure that having her write a few words and signing her name to them would shield me from the penalties the purists in our profession would throw at me, however upon reaching the fork in the road, that was the path I took.

A moment later it was clear that no judge would ever accuse me of succumbing to prurient interests. Her distress was very real, unfortunately, but for all the right reasons.

She had invited the intervention of a surgeon, recommended by a friend, to insert silicone implants in a manner that promised to improve upon nature. My eyes fell upon three longitudinal garish gashes, thickly swollen, dark red to an angry purple, that led to the nipple – which was itself surrounded by these same unholy swellings.

"Well you have to give it time to heal. I'm sure the surgeon told you this."

"He butchered me. The fuck butchered me for life. Where did he put my nipple?"

She asked a fair question. Somehow the nipple on her right breast was fixed in a position where it could communicate comfortably with her right armpit.

"Right now it does seem a wee bit too far to one side, but that could be as a result of the swelling. You simply can't rush things. You have to give it a chance to heal."

"He botched the job, didn't he!" The words weren't meant to sound as a question. "I'll sue the fucking asshole for everything he has."

"I'm not in a position where my opinion can count for much" I ventured weakly. "I don't think the operation was really necessary to begin with. Believe me, all a man really wants from a woman's breast is enough to fill the palm of his hand." This was pure invention, but I was at a loss for a more educated reply.

"You don't know much, do you!" She said getting to her feet. I half expected an expletive with regard to me.

"Sit down, Janet. There's more we have to talk about." And almost as an afterthought, "What if your lawyer will refuse to look at your breasts?"

"He's already seen them. Not everyone is a stuffed dick like you."

31

7. Swallowing

By the time Janet had reached her thirties she had fallen madly, I should say "desperately," in love with about as many men as a dozen healthy women would have felt about the men they had known in their lifetimes. Possibly an exaggeration but, then again, perhaps not. She was determined to have a life partner at her side – someone who would genuinely love her, be responsible for her (as she would be for him) – someone who would give her life measures of stability, meaning and direction. She would be everything he would want her to be.

Her natural creative talents and her way with Photoshop led to a successful career as a graphic designer. When we had our session she was at her third place of work. The owners of the first and second had been her lovers for a time, and when they lost interest in her sexually, she found herself on the way out. Albeit, she left with excellent references and letters of recommendation, but the doors slamming behind her exposed her yet again to the fickle tempers and hollow promises of her suitors. Her first employer was (and remained) married, but had sworn with hand on heart that a divorce was less than a month away. The second lived apart from his wife so that her nights with him at his home quite reassured her of his intentions. Until, of course, it was over. It wasn't long afterwards that he had, in fact, divorced his wife (or she him) but he quickly rebounded to a blond with hair that bounced off her shoulders – a nubile, double jointed, cheerleader on the varsity football team, and twenty one years his junior. All this she had learned from her third employer.

In truth she never lacked a man at her side. On one solo vacation she took to the Island of Crete she hitched herself to a man ahead of her in line for their boarding passes, and another to Dubrovnik where, on the plane, she found herself next to an alpha male tattooed owner of a cafe there. It was a long night flight, they had the row to themselves, and under a shared blanket she felt his warm hand make its way to her nether region. At first, feeling uncertain and confused, she shifted away from him with a meek "no". But his hand remained where it was and she soon relaxed. He had his way with her through the night without them leaving their seats. She remembered him a being absolutely her most exciting lover ever.

The issue of suffering the departure of all the "serious" men in her life had become central to everything that mattered to her. As a neurotic obsession it overtook even her nervous system judging from the occasional tic that was there at the corner of her mouth, and from the way her knee sometimes bounced off the ball of her foot in nervous, rat-a-tat spasms. I had asked her if she had any idea why the men would move away from her with what, almost invariably, seemed like out-of-the blue suddenness.

"Not a clue. Not a single clue. And it's always when I think things couldn't possibly be better... it's always when I'm feeling totally happy." Then, almost as an afterthought... "Motherfucking sons of bitches, all of them!"

"Are you careful with your personal hygiene?"

"You mean washing up and stuff?"

"Just asking... let's get this possibility behind us."

Plainly annoyed and showing some impatience with me she answered crisply. "I shower 2-3 times a day. I'm super careful with my private parts. I'm always in clean clothes, I brush my teeth, floss, and rinse with a mouthwash. What more do you want? I'm completely sterilized 24 hours of the day!"

"I believe you. I never thought differently. But you and I know that hidden somewhere are the answers we're looking for. We just have to find them."

"That's why I'm here. Right?"

"It's something we'll have to do together, Janet."

"That's why I'm here. Right?" With that came another tic and a bouncing knee spasm.

"You say it always happens... that they seem always to leave you... when you are convinced things couldn't be any better between the two of you."

"I never say no to anything they ask of me."

"Oh?"

"Never."

"Can you give me some idea what they might ask of you? Maybe we can find some answers here."

"I don't think so. I say "yes" to everything they want and they love me even more. Besides, it's too personal to talk about."

"It may help us both if you would. Try."

"Use your imagination." Again the tic and again the spasm.

"Does it have anything to do with oral sex?" This wasn't entirely a stab in the dark. I figured Janet hadn't invented anything that hadn't been popular since the days of Sodom and Gomorrah.

"Sometimes." It was the voice of a tiny mouse.

"And you let them ejaculate in your mouth?"

"They beg me to let them." The hesitant mouse wasn't there this time.

"And you swallow?"

After an extended pause and a deep breath, "They beg me to let them."

"And you let them."

"I let them".

"And you are OK with that? I queried.

"It tastes god awful, but what makes them happy really makes me happy."

"That's also the answer to the question you're asking. No man will want to spend his life with a woman who drinks his sperm."

"How can you say that?"

"Trust me."

Then, almost as an afterthought, Janet added: "And I thought maybe it was because I would also let them go in the back way."

8. "Look between my legs."

L ook here, right here between my legs. Do you see any light coming through?"

Cynthia was a somewhat heavyset girl, just turned twenty, with inch long green and yellow fingernails, silver lipstick and silver-green eye shadow. She wore a loose fitting, oversized tee-shirt on which was emblazoned the message *Milk My Love*. It might have been *Love My Milk*. I can't be sure. But I remember well the fingernails and the layers of paint on her face.

I also remember her rising from her chair, pulling up a short length of that tee-shirt, and pointing to the general area of her lady parts. She was wearing skin tight jeans, threatening to burst at the seams, and, judging from the length of the heels, shoes that were decidedly not sensible.

I learned that Cynthia had subscriptions to about a dozen fashion magazines. She also had a wardrobe with outfits that she could wear for well over a month without ever having to wear anything twice. But that was what she had in her wardrobe. On a day-to-day basis it was mostly these tight jeans with tee-shirts, with messages evidently inspired by Zen philosophers on crack.

Again. "Look. Do you see any light from behind me?"

Actually I was facing her so she might have translated her thoughts into words a tad more successfully. But I understood what she meant. What so disturbed her was that when standing with her legs together her generous thighs so pressed against each other that no light could squeeze between them. For Cynthia this was the end of the world. There was absolutely nothing meaningful that might await her in the bleakest tomorrows to come. She was doomed, hopelessly doomed, to live a life that would never know true love or romance.

She withdrew from her stylish patched tote bag a fashion magazine bedecked with people in all manner of dress and togetherness. There were enough smiles just on the cover to melt the icecaps. With a rigid index finger she drew my attention to a number of anorectic starlets in thongs that faced the camera, all standing with their legs together. Sure enough there was enough space under their vulvas for the Orient Express and all the Kentucky Derby horses to pass through without touching the sides – and all at the same time.

"You can't be serious." I ventured, unsure how to best address her distress.

"Well I AM SERIOUS! I am MORE than serious. I might just as well be dead."

"Those fashion magazines guarantee that any woman reading them will convince herself that she's ugly. Can you live on a carrot and a half a day? Those women swallow toilet paper to keep those figures."

"You know from nothing." Madly Cynthia flipped page after page. Finally she found what she was after and pushed the magazine almost to my face. "Does that look like carrots and toilet paper to you???"

On that page were photographs of a celebrity wedding with these starlets supposedly feasting on the creations of a master chef. Some held tall wine glasses toasting the bride over the sumptuous dishes in front of them. Others were shown biting delicately into prawns, garlic-buttered lobster, or goose-liver pate on thin toast. Admittedly it fell short of an imperial feeding orgy in Caligula's time, but not by much.

We shared a few more exchanges but it was clear that nothing I said had tempered her mood or frame of mind. I chose a more delicate, intimate tack – not particularly smart, just delicate and probably dumb – half convinced that I was about to bang a few nails into my own coffin.

"When you are out on the street I suppose you notice couples walking along together, sometimes arm in arm. Not so?"

"And not all of the women are thin. That's what you want to tell me?"

"Are all of the men fat, ugly slobs with pimples on their noses?"

"Some."

"But not all" I added, looking at her sternly, with narrowing eyebrows.

"So…?"

The point I want to make is that maybe what attracts the man to the woman is more than seeing a light coming through her legs.

"You mean like money?"

"No. I don't mean like money, (a long pause) I mean like sex… great sex!"

"Sell me another story."

"My problem," I said, half speaking to myself, "is that I'm not comfortable talking about this with someone – a girl – and one as young as you."

"I'm not that young. And you're just looking for a way out. No one will want sex with a hippopotamus."

I couldn't stop a short laugh escaping me, but I was genuinely angry at myself for that. That line was like a flashing neon sign. There was half a textbook on psychology buried in it.

"You have it all wrong, all wrong, and that's a shame. You haven't given yourself half a chance to gain some real life experience."

"I'm not a virgin if that's what you were thinking."

"No, that's not what I was thinking. But it makes what I want to say just a bit easier."

Silence. I continued – treading as delicately as I could with my words. "For a man, the good feeling he gets is when he feels he's a real man when having sex."

She was waiting for more. I plowed my mind to find the right words. "He will always have that feeling if he feels it's tight inside her." I was reducing myself to the level of a fifteen year old. "What I mean to say is that those super thin women, with all that open space between their thighs, can never give a man the same feeling a fuller bodied woman can. It's no secret. They may be much thinner but their – er – openings – are always much wider, never tight. You honestly have no reason to complain. You have to give yourself a chance."

With that she collected her things, left some bills on the table, never looking at me, and left. I never heard from her again.

9. One Hot Dog

Marcia lived with her boyfriend and Charlie, her German Shepherd, a ten minute walk from the ocean. Studying English Literature in her second year at college she enjoyed a convenient schedule that allowed her abundant free time. Her boyfriend was a bank clerk and their hours were comfortably regimented.

Charlie was a chronic humper. Marcia would laugh and free her leg with expressions of annoyance, but Charlie seemed determined. They had a ritual where returning from the ocean Marcia would soap and shower Charlie and then shower herself. On one occasion as she stepped out of the shower holding her towel, the cellphone on her bed started up.

As she lay belly down on her bed, her knees on the floor and with the phone at her ear, Charlie made his move. With one hand Marcia turned to one side and roughly pushed him away. The moment she was back on her belly Charlie was again over her.

Still in the thick of conversation Marcia, without thinking, slightly raised her backside and Charlie immediately attacked. His luck didn't hold and he kept missing the target area. Feigning annoyance with the world, Marcia ended her conversation, and even more roughly again pushed Charlie off her.

But something had stirred within her. She looked at her unquiet, lascivious dog and felt a tad sorry for him. This time she slowly laid down on the bed with Charlie following her. She raised her pelvis even higher than before, spread her legs, buried her head in the blanket and waited.

Charlie was an impatient novice, but with perseverance, much ambition and determination it happened. Marcia felt him penetrate her in a mad rush, knot and all. Afterwards she didn't mind having to wait for the swelling to go down. Her thoughts were on what she had permitted to happen, and how her body had taken to the experience.

She remembered the first time she saw dogs copulating. She was in the park with her best friends at the time, and they had to explain to her what the dogs were up to. She was only nine or ten years old then, but she remembered them telling her, between giggles, that one day she would be doing just what they were doing. She also remembered wondering what the girl dog could be feeling.

Charlie, to all intents and purposes, had become her lover. She got thick woolen stockings for his front paws. The moment Marcia went for those socks his excitement would sometimes have him ejaculate freely. He became very practiced, and as odd as it may sound, in Marcia's mind they were very much a couple in love.

Marcia's boyfriend was never the wiser, but he would increasingly complain that their lovemaking was too infrequent and invariably over too quickly. She complained about the demands of her college courses. She did what she could to keep him with her as his salary covered the rent. However, love and passion, she knew, would no longer be in the equation of their relationship.

When Marcia visited me her single concern was to learn whether she was normal. Her eyes were awash in tears.

10. Sacrifice and Double Play

Married less than a week, they came to the big city from a small, slow-motion, farming community about 300 miles away. It was their ambition to find, somewhere in the rich possibilities of the loud, hustle and bustle of the metropolis, a new and more promising life for themselves. They were both 23 years old, some high school education, and with enough money between them to cover cheap lodgings and two months of groceries at the very most.

They scanned the help-wanted sections in every newspaper, and looked in every storefront window for a place that might offer work. They appreciated that their resumes – she, strong on growing tomatoes and he, beekeeping – would find scant mention in the want ads, but they were open to learning and to what Jason, the husband, described as "reinventing" themselves.

Eleanor thought she might find work in a restaurant kitchen. Jason expected that his frame was strong enough to lend itself to work at jobs that needed physical effort. Among their less serious problems at that time was with their iron wrought bed which squeaked loudly, and especially so, during their frequent lovemaking. As they could hear the goings-on in the flat on the other side of their bedroom wall they knew they were not holding back any secrets from their neighbors. They resolved this problem by setting the mattress on the floor.

When job hunting they would split. One morning Eleanor answered an ad for help in the kitchen of a popular restaurant in the heart of the city. She went early enough to catch one of the owners with time to spare. He was at a table chatting with a meticulously dressed man in a dark suit with matching vest and yellow-green striped tie. The owner, decidedly overweight, was in an oversized shirt emblazoned with tropical trees and a smiling tropical girl, falling carelessly over his trousers.

She was invited to join them at the table, but when the owner was shown their ad and heard her out he told her to return in an hour when the chef would be there. The kitchen was his department. As she got up to leave the man with him smiled at her and handed her his card. "I'm at city hall," he said, "if things don't go well with the chef give me a call". Eleanor took the card and returned the smile. This was turning out to have all the makings of a new kind of day.

The chef wanted someone with kitchen experience, and growing tomatoes fell short of what he could live with. Less than three minutes after they met she found herself back on the sidewalk. Her mood crashed, but only for the moment.

While waiting for the hour to pass she had studied the card handed to her. The embossed city emblem at a corner of the card seemed to invest the card with much promise. The man seemed to be in a high administrative office. As they could only afford one cellphone between them which stayed with Jason, Eleanor dropped a precious quarter in a phone box and called him.

As a 23 year old in a large city, seeking employment that came with a wage packet that might help cover rent and the economics of daily life, he found himself on the end of a bitter education. He was given to understand that many workplaces preferred Blacks, Mexicans, or Puerto Ricans over pale skinned Caucasians. Where a job was available the salary offered wouldn't have covered the expense of a week's groceries. He tried heavy truck moving companies only to learn that he hadn't the frame to lift refrigerators off the ground, let alone up three flights of stairs. Wherever he turned it seemed that there would always be a reason for the doors to remain locked before him.

Eleanor's message brought with it a spark of encouragement, although he advised her not to get her hopes up too high.

She invested another quarter to call the number on the card. To the first voice she gave the extension. To the second her name. A moment later the same voice asked whether she had an appointment as he was presently in a meeting. No she hadn't, but she was calling at the request of that gentleman. Could she offer any further details? "He gave me his card this morning at the "Steer Way" restaurant) and asked me to call him. He said it would be OK to call him."

Suddenly "Eleanor. Is that you? Eleanor?" Apparently his meeting ended with marvelous abruptness. "Yes sir. The chef wanted a more experienced girl." They arranged to meet the following morning at the same restaurant. She would join him for breakfast.

He was intensely interested in learning about her life on the farm, the varieties of tomatoes they grew, how they were marketed, and what she was looking for in big city life. She spoke of the difficulties she and Jason were encountering trying to secure a foothold in the city with the little money they brought with them.

Sam Patterson was his name. Outside the office she could call him Sam, but if she got into the office it would have to be "Mr. Patterson."

"Oh yes. Mr. Patterson."

"Sam."

He told her that he needed someone he could trust… that he needed a diligent, keen eyed person to manage the inbox-outbox material which was now the size of a mountain, and when other responsibilities left little time for his other office people to manage. Eleanor held back asking what an inbox-outbox was and badly suffered her ignorance, but she kept her silence. He went on to say that he needed this person to work closely with him – sometimes after hours, and sometimes even to travel with him, to manage his papers at out-of-town conferences, and would that be alright with her husband. He was looking directly into her eyes. The starting pay packet she would be bringing home would come to $60 K a year, but, depending on how seriously she identified with him, and her efficiency with her office work, it could reach $80 K within two years.

Eleanor's head was spinning. She was to begin working at the start of the month, which was little more than a week away. In the meantime she was to show up at the office to fill out the employment forms and to have one of his staff explain the nature of her responsibilities with the inbox-outbox material. Had she died at that moment it would have been from happiness.

It took a heavy weight off Jason's mind, but he wasn't entirely sure what out-of-town conferences would demand of Eleanor. The question annoyed her. She assured him that there couldn't possibly be anything to worry about as he was a very serious person in a hugely important position, married, much respected, older than her father, and with a daughter older than herself. Their lovemaking that night was rich with joy.

At the office she was given a tag. That gave Eleanor her first feeling of being a legitimate part of the army of busy people so at home in the building. It was a precious feeling. Peggy, a dark girl under an intricate African-American braid hairstyle, was given the chore of showing her around and introducing her to the work expected of her. The inbox was where all the material that needed attention would accumulate. In effect it wasn't a box at all but three sets of files in both alphabetical order and dating order that took up an entire filing cabinet. The outbox wasn't a filing cabinet but material collected on a shelf that required distribution to other offices, mostly to the legal people, the accounting people and the public relations people – all on different floors. There was nothing here over her head. She had a cubicle to herself. That it was next to the washroom never disturbed her. The only thing that somehow did disturb her was Sam Patterson making several exits from his office without once looking in her direction. "Had he had second thoughts?" She wondered.

At the start of her second week he asked her to kindly fetch the files that belonged to a specific legal claim on the city.

She knew exactly the files he wanted and where to find them. Clutching them as a schoolgirl clutches her books she returned to the room in swift strides and abundant self-confidence.

With the door to his office closed behind her the cold and distant Mr. Patterson morphed back into the warm and friendly Sam.

"How are you feeling with us, Eleanor? Is everything OK?

"Oh, much more than OK. I love the work, and I love the people here."

"Does that include me?" He winked at her.

Eleanor felt the blood rush to her cheeks, but she look squarely into his eyes. "Oh yes, Mr. Patterson, it begins with you most of all."

He smiled almost to himself. "I think we'll get along just fine."

He withdrew a few documents from the files and asked her to give them to another girl to attach transcripts of phone conversations to them. But then, almost as an afterthought, he added, "I'd like you at 7 pm tonight to meet me in the lobby of the Benjamin Hotel. I'll want your opinion on this file. Do you think you can make it?"

Eleanor froze.

"A problem with your husband?

Her mind became a tangle of thoughts, but her survival instincts came through. "No. I'll be there." But she felt as though her knees were gone.

"Great. Take the file home, don't lose any papers, study it, and bring it with you."

Jason wasn't at all comfortable with their hotel meeting which, to his mind, seemed like an assignation unrelated to her office work. He was having a dreadful time, suffering failure after failure, in his search for work. The sense of impotence delivered him to the edge of depression. At the same time he could not help noticing how Eleanor would walk taller and with longer strides than ever before. Before his eyes she seemed to have distanced herself from the tomato patches by measures less in miles that in heart and mind.

Sam Patterson showed no interest in the files that Eleanor had studied so intently. She had arrived a few minutes before he did, and being alone on the leather chair in that small lobby quite unnerved her. But then he came through the doors and she got to her feet to greet him. They found a table at the far corner of the lobby and ordered coffees.

"I'll tell you in all honesty why I called you here," he began, tapping his teaspoon on the saucer. "It has nothing to do with your work in the office, which, I'm told, is A One... A One," he repeated.

Eleanor nodded her thanks, but she felt as though at the edge of an abyss. He continued.

"It has to do with you personally. I was really glad you called and I was happy to give you this job, not only because it was available, but because I liked you from the start." He paused and studied her carefully. Eleanor neither moved nor uttered a sound. He continued.

"Now I'm going to say something. I'll be as direct as I can. You don't have to agree and you can walk away from here as though this meeting never happened. I will think nothing of it and no mention of it will be made ever. But I was thinking that arrangements could be made to find employment with the city for your husband at a pretty good salary. Really, and at a decent salary. It all depends if you and I can get closer."

"I don't know what you mean Mr. Patterson. I don't know what to say."

"Sam."

"Sam."

"Well I'll leave you to think about it. We're talking English, not Chinese." With that he wrote a number on a napkin and pushed it in her direction. "That's my room number here. I'll leave you now and you can take your time to decide whether to join me in the room, which would please me very much, or (removing a crisp $20.00 bill from his wallet and setting it near her cup) you can take a cab home." With that he rose from his chair, took the files Eleanor had with her, and walked to the elevators. He didn't look back.

Less than five minutes later she knocked softly on the door to his room.

A few days later Jason came for his appointment with Mr. Patterson. Together they went down to a basement area where all the printed material related to the municipality was stored. Inside an office there Jason was introduced to the man who gave him his job at the printing presses at the city's industrial zone. It wasn't very far from where Eleanor and Jason were presently living.

Eleanor and her boss would have their tryst at least once a week. He always had a room somewhere. Most often they would use the lunch hour, and if their lovemaking carried beyond that hour it troubled no one. They never left the office together nor ever returned together. On occasion, the hotel venue at 7 pm was where they spent an hour or two. The stickiest hours with Jason came when her boss wanted her to accompany him to a 3 day conference in London. When Jason complained Eleanor, almost in anger, assured him that it was 100% work, that two other people from the office were joining them, and that they all had separate rooms. In her heart she felt bitter and resentful of Jason who would never know how much of herself she had sacrificed for him.

In fact she alone had accompanied Sam Patterson, but she did have a room in her name and when Jason would call, even with her away, she would find the message and call him back. Each time she complained to him about how many hours she had to invest in going through the documents, but that, all in all, it was fun. And that Sam Patterson was a perfect gentleman.

This arrangement between Sam Patterson, Eleanor and Jason carried on for just over two years. The couple had moved out of their original flat and found another in a newer building, and one very comfortably furnished. On several occasions, with Jason at work, Eleanor and her boss would have their hour and some there. But things weren't the same for the couple. There were frequent outbursts of annoyance and anger with the distance between them increasing steadily. Sex between them became less and less frequent, devoid of any trace of passion, and increasingly mechanical. Their financial circumstances, however, permitted investments in clothes, fine restaurants and the occasional play or artistic performance when they would pay over $500.00 for each ticket. They made several friends and would meet at a popular bar. This was their life, that is, until it was over.

Sam Patterson went to prison for embezzlement and corruption having received bribes for building contracts, and bribes for services to the city – specifically garbage collection, that altogether came to more than ten million dollars kept in Swiss banks and offshore islands. There were also serious tax evasion penalties. Eleanor and Jason were both fired.

The couple divorced. Jason returned to his beekeeping and his quiet community life. Eleanor remained in the city certain she now had the tools, the experience, the acquaintances, in sum the wherewithal, to find her way again. Her thoughts sometimes returned to Sam Patterson. She missed him. Jason might never have existed.

11. Becoming Dirty

Judith was seven, in the second grade when her story began. She had forgotten her glasses in the hall where her class had exercised a few minutes earlier. With her teacher's permission she returned to the hall but her glasses weren't where she was certain she had left them. A moment later she saw a delivery man a few yards away smiling at her. He had a package under one arm, but with the other he showed her the glasses and asked if this was what she was looking for.

Oh, yes. She ran to him with her arm outstretched but he held back saying that she would have to pay him with a kiss on his cheek. "No," she said. So, still smiling, he started to walk away with her glasses. She ran after him. He turned, bent down as she made a kissing sound in the air. At that, he handed her the glasses, smiled a friendly smile, and walked off with the package.

Judith raced back to her classroom and excitedly shared an account of this encounter with all her little friends. But a moment later, when the teacher interrupted them, it was quickly forgotten.

Judith then returned home. It was a day like every other day. She had her lunch, played with a friend and later in the afternoon took her bath. As she washed her, her mother asked what she had learned that day. In the stream of her recollections of that day, Judith remembered the experience with her glasses and shared that experience with her mother with the same excited, almost joyful lilt in her voice that she did with her friends.

To Judith's horror, she saw her mother pale visibly. Shaking the girl by her shoulders, her mother insisted that she tell her everything – *but everything... absolutely everything* – that the man had done to her.

Judith was frightened and found herself unsure of what to say. "He started to walk away with my glasses. He wouldn't give them to me if I didn't give him a kiss."

"A kiss? What do you mean a kiss? A kiss where? A kiss to a strange man? Did he touch you? Think! Think! Where did he touch you?"

Judith began to cry. She was as confused as she was frightened. Her mother dried her roughly, dressed her, and raged. "Why didn't you just run away? Why didn't you shout? Did you ever see him before? Did he do anything with himself?" With that she went for the phone and called her father.

"Come home immediately. I want to go the school even at this hour. There was a man who did things to Judith. I can't get anything out of her." Her father appeared looking as distraught as her mother. He wanted to know if the man had opened his trousers. He wanted to know whether he had touched her between her legs. By this time Judith was crying so hysterically she had to struggle to catch her breath. Words could not reach her lips.

The principal was still at the school and the account in the gym was repeated again and again. Her parents wanted to know how the teacher could permit the child to go unaccompanied to the gym. The principal was at a loss and suggested that the parents register a complaint with the police. And that's where they went.

A female officer spoke with Judith and used a doll to get Judith to tell her just what the man had done to her. Judith's flowing tears, frightened eyes and difficulty speaking seemed only to confirm the mother's suspicions. But a short while later tempers cooled somewhat and Judith described once again the account with the man that no one seemed to believe or understand. The officer then assured the parents that they had overreacted, and that had they listened to their daughter they would have understood that the incident was entirely innocent. The mother listened, still unsure what to believe. She sternly and bitterly castigated Judith once again for letting this happen. Days passed. The incident was forgotten and her mother never mentioned it again. But what Judith carried away with her from this experience was that she was unclean and undeserving of anything from anybody. She had dirtied herself, shamed herself, and utterly defiled herself. This was who she was, and how she would forever be.

Years went by and Judith matured into an attractive woman. At the age of twenty-eight she married a violent psychotic who twice had beaten her to that proverbial "inch of her life". Her friends could never understand her insistence that he really loved her, that she deserved the battering, repeating yet again that it was her fault, and that she would never ever leave him.

12. Nothing to Wear

Bev (born Beverly) was 38 when I met her. Her carrot red hair was cropped very short, and long tangled configurations of silver wire hung from her ears very nearly reaching her shoulders. She was decidedly overweight. Her breasts under her stylish black dress were ample. but sitting in her chair the rolls of fat at her stomach pressed up against them, diminishing their size and making a convenient rest for her folded arms.

She was not unattractive. Her lips were sharply defined and her cheeks were softly dimpled. A small and somewhat receding chin suggested a certain vulnerability and (the cropped hair notwithstanding) it somehow accented her femininity. Her eyes were clear and sharply focused under thin and highly arched eyebrows.

Bev was married to a successful accountant and they had three children – all girls. The oldest was nine, the second eight and the youngest two. She had a law degree but never practiced law apart from the year she was required to spend as an apprentice in a law office. She complained that the whole business of law left her cold and uninspired – something that she should have expected from the start. Choosing law was definitely a mistake, she said, and if her intelligence and long hours of study had delivered good grades through the years, those grades offered no solace for the overwhelming sense of emptiness that soon came to weigh heavily upon her. Later she tried her hand at journalism and had invested considerable sums in courses before finding herself, again, overtaken by the feeling that she was merely deceiving herself. Journalism was not for her – despite several pieces she had written on labor issues that were well received. She was quite upset at the license the editors had permitted themselves when editing her material. She complained of feeling that her published material, at least the material that carried her name, had all the color and texture, not to mention the taste, of waxed fruit.

There was a period of several months where she worked in an advertising agency. She left that to open a pastry shop in partnership with another woman. That enterprise failed when the two women could not find common ground on their respective contributions to the enterprise, or even on the shop's interior design.

It was at about this time that she met her husband. He was the son of her father's accountant and they met at the wedding of his older brother. Through connections her husband's family had with a large real-estate firm she was taken on by them as a sales agent. On her very first week she recorded enormous success and she let herself believe that at last she had found her natural setting in life. The people she had to deal with were friendly, intelligent, sophisticated, often well-read and worldly. She had access to a company car and enjoyed perks that went beyond anything she might have hoped for.

Midway through the pregnancy with her first child, she left the company. Her income was nice but not a critical factor in the economics of their household. She admitted to having had no regrets about leaving her job. It was nice while it lasted, and it was convenient, but nothing more.

Bev said she loved her husband. She meant this sincerely even though two weeks before their marriage she spent a full weekend in a hotel room with a man she had met only a day or two earlier. Her cover was a program at that hotel where people were taught how to meditate, how to cleanse their bodies with enemas and fruit juice, and how to ward off potential health disorders by coordinating body-mind experiences. The participants were committed to silence and forbidden even to answer the phone. It was all there in the brochure that she had hurriedly shown to her parents and fiancé.

She said that the sexual excitement and passion she had experienced at that tryst was far more powerful than anything she had ever known with her forever understanding, and always accommodating husband. She needed that experience, she said, to feel that she was still alive. After the wedding she turned down that man's suggestion that they meet again. Nevertheless, the thought that she still occupied his attentions and that he still wished an intimate moment with her pleased her as much as it surprised her.

Years later she did allow herself another sexual relationship although it proved as disappointing as it was short-lived. It was with her older daughter's riding instructor. He was from France and she thought of all the secrets he would share with her in bed together. That, at least, was the promise in his eyes. It was a promise that never carried through to the bed. She could recall, ruefully, how he would not once look at her, or utter a sound during the three or four minutes that they copulated. She cried, she said, for days on end, and had no explanation for continuing to bring her daughter to his lessons. What was even worse and quite terrible, she confessed, was that if he had wanted to be with her a second time, she would readily have agreed.

She had been married for about four years when she was diagnosed as suffering from some minor metabolic problem. This explained her weight gain she said, and try as she might to reduce, whether by pills, acupuncture, exercise, or all three together, her success was limited at best.

Now she wanted to leave her domestic rituals and return to some form of employment or study. She had to do something... *anything*. Otherwise she risked becoming like her mother, who could never experience joy... who would forever complain about having given up her life for others. She recalled how as a child, hardly a day would pass that she would not hear her mother, prone to shrieking, threaten to walk out the door and just disappear... that no one in her life ever did anything for her. In her heart Bev just knew the words were meant for her... that she had been her mother's bad fortune and greatest disappointment.

Exactly what area of work or study might appeal to her wasn't at all clear in her mind. In the past she had tried so many things and showed promise in so many fields, but at no time did she ever feel for any length of time a vital attachment to where she was, or to what she was doing – even in her marriage. Her feeling was not unlike what would overtake her when rummaging through all her expensive outfits and finding she had nothing to wear. For a time she considered divorcing her husband. Their sex life had come to a virtual standstill inasmuch as she had repeated fantasies of being raped and of otherwise being violated physically and sexually. In this her husband was incapable of accommodating her. But she would never divorce him, probably for the same reasons her mother never divorced her father.

13. Couldn't Say "No"

Laura, single at twenty-six, lived alone with her pet dog in a small town near the Canadian border, a stone's throw from Burlington in the State of Vermont. She lost her father when she was twenty years old, and her mother when she was twenty-two. To support herself, she worked at the local post office. She was quiet, modest, unassuming, and very conscientious. She dressed carefully and took to growing roses in a patch of earth around the front and south side her house.

Laura had one brother living in a town between Burlington and Montpellier, which was about fifty kilometers west of her town. A frequent bus service connected between the two towns, and because he had a family with several children it was more convenient for her to visit him than for him to visit her. On one such visit, a Saturday, he had another visitor, a school friend from a town not far from where Laura lived.

Laura didn't much like this friend. She didn't like his language, his squeaky laughter, the way he smoked his cigarettes, or the untidy way he carried himself. She had met him about a year earlier and reacted negatively to him even then. When it came time to leave, the friend offered to take her home in his panel truck since her town was along the same highway that took him to his own town. Laura at first said "no", but weakly. Her brother, her sister-in-law, and the fellow himself soon convinced her to accept the offer.

All along the way, the fellow told her stories about his success with women, and how he thought the two of them could really be something great together. He was carried away, seemingly convinced by his own enthusiasm it seems. All the while, Laura remained silent. When he put his arm around her shoulder she froze, but said nothing. This seemed to encourage him even more, and he waxed almost philosophical in his attempt to convince her to let them have a few minutes together. Laura could not utter a word.

He turned off the road and into a thick grove of maple trees. It was early Fall, the sap was too early to tap so they were quite alone. In a small clearing he cut the motor and opened his trousers. In her mind, Laura was shouting, "No," and again, "No," and again, "No," until it was over.

Then he drove her to her door and continued on his way. She collected her dog from a neighbor, fed it, and then took a taxi to the police station in Burlington. There she complained of being raped. The police drove with her to where he had turned off the road into the forest of trees. They found the clearing and there, on the ground, the crumpled tissues with the semen. At three in the morning they reached the fellow at his home and brought him to their station.

He repeated almost word for word everything that Laura had complained of. But he added that not once had she resisted – neither with words nor with actions. "Not once did she ask me to stop." The police asked Laura if this was true. "Yes," she admitted. "He didn't give me a chance to say no." The police let him go, expressing their apologies.

I met Laura for the first time about half a year later as a referral from her therapist. She was still in the throes of a serious depression in the wake of that experience, and talked more frequently about taking her life.

I don't know what became of her. Her therapist had returned to South Africa so I couldn't learn anything from that quarter. I did learn, however, that her father had been a cold, hard hearted and very brutal man who dominated their lives and demanded that everything be done in exactly the fashion he would dictate. There was no contradicting him, arguing with him or turning a back on him. He was not averse to striking their faces. At one point her brother had spent several months in jail for threatening to shoot him. The father had reported him to the authorities and a subsequent search uncovered an unlicensed weapon. It was the property of her father who told the police it was the property of his son. The son never challenged him.

14. Free Floating and Rudderless

Marlene was born in Austria but lived in Toronto from the age of two. Her parents had divorced when she was six. She lived with her mother who soon remarried. Her father had meanwhile returned to Austria. When she visited me Marlene was twenty-six.

A slight girl, almost anorectic, she wore her pale blond hair in long, thin, tightly plaited dreadlocks that terminated in an assortment of wooden and plastic beads. A thin necklace of tiny black beads, which I was later told were genuine Tahitian pearls, was strung around her neck. She dressed with a studied carelessness – a thin, loosely hanging, collarless pink blouse tucked into fraying denim shorts. On her feet were gladiator sandals with long leather strips laced in crisscross fashion halfway to her knees.

She left high-school at the age of 16. With the few hundred dollars she had saved – gifts from her father, in the main – she left for Vienna where she imagined her father would introduce her to a world of possibilities that would otherwise never be known to her. Certainly not in Toronto where everything began and ended with the income bracket a person belonged to.

Her father accepted her with genuine enthusiasm until she gave him to understand that her immediate plans did not include returning to her mother whom she described as being pathologically selfish – a "user." Neither would she be returning to school – not in Toronto and not in Vienna. He wasn't a wealthy man, and he tried as tactfully as possible to have her understand that he was ill-prepared to support her indefinitely. He also had certain obligations to a woman with whom he shared most of his time. It was evident that he was pained when she registered her disappointment, but at that moment Austria became as foreign to Marlene as the moon. She knew, with absolute certainty, that at that moment she was taking her final leave of her father – that his home, Vienna, indeed Austria, would never be more than those stations with unremembered names that the trains rush by in the thick of night.

She returned to Toronto and worked as a waitress in a coffee shop. A close friendship developed with another girl who worked there, and the latter introduced her to her small circle of friends. One fellow was in acting school and did part-time bartending; another was a sound technician. They, in turn, introduced her to marijuana and the distance from there to their beds was short. A girl in that group had ambitions as a singer and was forever on the phone with her agent. She spoke well of the possibility of earning considerable sums of money in Japan, and they met with another girl who had just returned from Osaka and who was going back there just as soon as she could be sure of receiving her share of her recently deceased father's estate.

Marlene became locked on the idea of finding something for herself in Japan. She merged with a network of young people who traveled through Asia and was able to get names and addresses of some who, she hoped, would help her find a foothold in Tokyo, Osaka or some other large Japanese city. After fifteen months at the coffee shop and perfectly familiar with what she called "soft drugs and hard sex" she turned her back on her friends, on everything familiar, and set out for Japan. She traveled alone with a few clothes, a passport, and just over one thousand US dollars tucked inside a money belt that the girl from Osaka had given her.

A little over two years later she returned to Toronto. She had accumulated over twenty thousand dollars, the bulk of which came from a very short association with an elderly banker whom she met while working as a hostess in a Tokyo club. She had accompanied him on trips to Singapore, London and Milan, flying first class and staying with him in the most luxurious suites. He was as good as his word and as generous to her with money as she was to him with her body. Their relationship came to an abrupt end when he registered his displeasure at her returning to her work at that club. His displeasure filtered through to the club's manager who quickly let her go. Before finding employment at the club, she had worked in street stalls selling pictures, ornaments, cosmetics, clothing accessories and jewelry. For the most part this work proved remunerative but it frequently annoyed the police and she constantly had to play cat and mouse with them. Not happy with the prospect of returning to those stalls and feeling she had had her full of hostessing, she left Japan with an American boy and they spent a month together in Bangkok and on some of the Thai islands. From there she returned alone to Toronto.

She considered the possibility of going back to school. But at the age of twenty-one, and with only the vaguest notions about what to do with her life, that seemed too long, too hard, and too uncertain a distance to cover. When in Thailand she played with the idea of purchasing local furniture and handicrafts and starting an import-export business with partners in Toronto and other countries. She decided, however, that she was not prepared to gamble with the money now in her pocket. She took a course in astrology thinking it might help her understand herself better, and from there went on to a course in graphology. About halfway through the latter, and feeling at a loss managing the myriad details, she decided she needed to focus far more carefully, and in a far more concrete and disciplined way on her future.

To that end she left for India and eventually linked up with a group making their way to Rishikesh. She loved the place and felt she could spend her life there. But after four months she suffered a psychotic episode when attending one of the many ashrams open to visitors. It seems that in following the strict regime set down by that ashram's guru, she went for long stretches without eating and without attending to her toilet. It brought to mind the brainwashing techniques depicted so brutally in *The Manchurian Candidate*. An uncle rushed to India to bring her back to Toronto. Marlene made that return flight a decidedly unpleasant experience for him. She was kept in a government psychiatric hospital for a short spell. Her condition improved and she continued her treatment there for a time as an out-patient.

After that Marlene thought that she might find her true vocation in hotel work. Not having completed high school she could not be accepted into any of the courses which the government tourist board offered. But her vibrant youthfulness, charming soft-spoken manner and her knowledge of languages, which now included a smattering of Japanese, apparently impressed the manpower people at a large hotel that belonged to an international chain. They gave her a position in the department that handled conventions and social affairs. The perks were marvelous and included a generous wardrobe allowance.

It was at a convention for dental surgeons that she met

Brian. He had remained in Toronto a month after the convention ended just to be with her. Marlene totally captivated his imagination and he was prepared to commit himself to a life that would include no other woman but her. They went to restaurants, discotheques and movies, but apart from warm embraces there was no sexual intimacy.

At thirty-two, Brian started balding which was not to Marlene's liking. Otherwise he might have been her perfect partner in life. He had his own clinic and was among the first to incorporate laser technology in his practice. He worked out regularly, played tennis and squash, jogged miles, and seemed very knowledgeable about wines and the whereabouts of all the fine restaurants of Provence. He owned his own home in New Jersey and drove a top-of-the-line Toyota. Before he left, he proposed marriage but told her he would wait until she came to the States to see what the nature of their life together would be like.

A month later she quit her job and flew to New Jersey. She agreed to stay in his home, which, indeed, was fine and luxurious, but in a room apart from his own. A week later she moved into his room, and not long after that there was a wedding. She had "pleaded" for a simple Reno marriage, but eventually accommodated his wishes for a more elaborate ceremony. He repaid her with a fast, sporty, two-seater Lancia.

74

Everyone thought they were the perfect couple. They played well together as tennis partners, and often had friends over for her Chinese, Japanese and Indian suppers. They were often seen holding hands and sharing private jokes. Then one day, without warning, she told him that she had met someone in a Manhattan bookstore and wanted to spend some time with him. Just like that and without once blinking! His reply was "How much time?" He still tried his mightiest to be understanding.

That tryst lasted one weekend. Marlene returned to New Jersey and their life continued just as before. They divorced two years later and she returned to Toronto. She was now a rather wealthy young woman of twenty-five with ambitions of opening and running her own coffee house. Instead, she registered for study at a well-known institute for fashion design. She quickly developed a friendship with a woman instructor there who was ten years her senior and they settled into a quiet lesbian relationship. At the same time she permitted herself a sexual relationship with that woman's husband – indeed with that woman's knowledge and blessing. From this union Marlene became pregnant and considered having the child. However, on the first week of her third month she had an abortion, which ended not only her pregnancy but her ambitions as a fashion designer. She wondered what her chances might be of getting her old job back at the hotel – not that she particularly cared to go back.

Shortly after her return to Toronto, Brian started calling her. almost begging her to come back, and have them start anew. She told him that their marriage was a gross mistake and that he could never be more than a friend to her. In her heart she knew that she didn't even want him as a friend. But then his calls stopped and Marlene learned that the daughter of one of New Jersey's most prominent families was seeing him frequently. Something stirred in her. When she later learned that they went on an extended vacation to some South Sea Islands and would be living together when they returned, she knew she wanted him back more than she had every wanted anyone or anything in her life.

15. Two Sides of the Same Coin

Paul was a regular guy. That's how he saw himself. He was a civil engineer, had a great income, drove a tar black 3.5 liter BMW, owned a designer-furnished condo on the 30th floor that boasted a genuine butcher's block, three washrooms, a sauna and jacuzzi. He was 42 years old, had all his hair, and was quite unmarried.

Paul enjoyed women and by every measure it seemed that women enjoy being with him. He was a familiar face at the "in" restaurants, always knowing what wines to order and how his dishes were to be prepared. At the social clubs he frequented he was never at a want for the attention of attractive company. His long-standing male friends were all married with children, and they make no secret of their envy of his relationships with girls twenty years his junior and fifteen to twenty years younger than their wives.

He made no secret of his wish to finally settle down with a woman he can love. And with every new relationship he seriously examined his feelings for her. After three or four times together in bed, however, he would again be overtaken by an all-too-familiar cloud of disappointment. It was nothing he could pinpoint. The girls might be marvelous cooks with killer bodies. With few exceptions, the sex was terrific – but something – some intangible – was invariably missing. At the right time he would make the appropriate and well-practiced noises while weakly discharging. She would smile, happily sharing the moment with him, but in fact he would feel nothing. In his heart he knew that she just couldn't be the woman he was searching for.

Tess was a popular fashion designer. The ideas came to her quickly and her strength was in anticipating correctly the styles and fabrics that will take off in the same season a year hence. She was also a frequent contributor to an important and popular fashion magazine, and, on occasion, emceed fashion shows.

She had married a childhood sweetheart when she was twenty-one and divorced him a few days short of their first anniversary. Since then she had had two very serious, if somewhat open relationships. The first lasted two years, and the second six. At the age of thirty-three she was positively chic. With a figure set off by long, mannequin legs, a swan's neck, high cheekbones, chiseled lips, a narrow waist and firm breasts.

Her suitors were all successful professional men who were sure enough about their own inherent worth not to be intimidated by her beauty, her intelligence, her position, her fame and her immaculate self-assuredness.

Appearances apart, Tess never had qualms about getting into bed with her partner, even if it was their first date. More often than not it was she who suggested he stay for breakfast. She wasn't one who believed in games, she'd say. It seemed her partners managed comfortably with this. One very impressive lady, they would think. A cut above all the other women they had ever known.

If there was a second date it would again end in the bedroom. However, no breakfast this time. And no third date.

Tess loved the undressing, the kissing, the embracing and especially the foreplay if it was inventive. But the actual penetration into her body left her quite numb, even uneasy. She could feel nothing. She would wait impatiently for her partner to pull away. Meanwhile her thoughts would carry in all directions save where she was, what she was doing and who she was doing it with.

Something was definitely missing.

By some peculiar alignment of the planets Paul and Tess had once met and had considered their options as lovers.

For whatever reason the subject had turned to childhood experiences. Paul had complained that his mother had never nurtured him as an infant... that she had always been sickly and that their bodies had never once met. It had always been an older sister that looked after him. Tess had tears in her eyes when she told Paul that her story was virtually identical to his, apart from the fact that her mother had had her at the age of sixteen. Attaching herself physically to another person had never been in her repertoire of early life experiences.

It had never been an experience that was there for either of them to repeat. Neither Paul nor Tess had any wish to meet beyond the two marvelously intimate evenings they had had having dinner together at a chef's restaurant.

16. Learning to Make the Right Noises

When Dorothy was born her father was already living apart from her mother. He was a stockbroker working in Manhattan and living in a loft he had rented there. He often said that the home he purchased with her mother in a small New Jersey town was exactly the home he wished to have when he retired, but that was when they married. It had spacious rooms, expansive lawns, and high bay windows behind white translucent drapes falling gracefully from the ceiling to the floor. Dorothy could also describe the rich mahogany table and chairs in their dining room (imported from Belgium), with mahogany chests with thick green marble tops (imported from Italy). She could remember all this because her mother would use every opportunity to tell her just how exclusive their home furnishings were, and how fortunate Dorothy should feel to live in this home.

Not two weeks after she was born, Dorothy's mother was back at her work selling cosmetics at a large department store. She was the manager of that counter, and explained that with her away sales had fallen considerably. She had hired a young live-in nursemaid to care for Dorothy, and it was in the arms of the nursemaid that Dorothy was brought home from the hospital. About a month later, the mother discovered that some of her earrings were missing, and after accusing the nursemaid of the theft she fired her. That very same day she hired another nursemaid, this time someone much older than the first. The following day she found the earrings but no apologies to the girl were forthcoming. ("Why give her an excuse to sue me?") The second nursemaid stayed with her for a few months until problems in her own family obliged her to leave them. Then came a third nursemaid, and after her a fourth.

All this Dorothy remembered from stories that her mother liked to repeat as though it was a history of some significance. Her mother would describe with some amusement her disgust at the thought of having to change Dorothy's diapers. ("I would die first.") She even seemed to relive the disgust that overcame her when once, holding Dorothy after the nursemaid had fed her, and Dorothy had vomited on the shoulder of the red chiffon designer dress she had bought the day before. ("I wanted to kill you.")

Dorothy's visits to her father were infrequent. She wasn't comfortable with his enthusiastic bear hugs and kisses, and she especially didn't like it when he mussed her hair. Also, he was living with a woman and Dorothy could not even bring herself to smile at her, let alone exchange pleasantries. Once she overheard her father apologize to his girlfriend. "Don't let it get to you. One day she'll grow up." Dorothy decided then never again to cross the threshold of his home.

When Dorothy had asked her mother why they divorced, her mother answered brightly: "He wanted something that I wouldn't give him." What that "something" was was left hanging in the air.

Dorothy's first sexual experience was at the age of sixteen. It was at a party in a large house, with a lot of drinking, pill popping, grass smoking, and loud, heavy, thumping music. They were mostly her classmates there, but each brought friends and the friends brought friends. The mood quickly shifted from polite, almost shy small talk to raucous laughter – and dancing that carried everyone on a veritable tsunami of sexual tension.

She fell onto a bed with a boy she had never met before and whose name she never knew. There was another couple on the bed at the time, completely naked, and they had happily invited the two into the room when they saw them gaping at them from the doorway.

Dorothy remembered the condom that her partner swung in the air to see how much he had ejaculated. He told her she was terrific and she returned the compliment. She knew, however, that she had felt nothing, absolutely nothing, not even a twitch of pain, even though she found spots of blood on the inside of her thigh. "Maybe my body was there," she said, "but I wasn't." Before the evening was over she got into the same bed with another boy. This time she recalled being more focused on what was happening. When that boy began struggling, almost angrily, to penetrate her, she broke away and dressed in a rush. Not long afterwards she staggered outside, doubled over on the grass and threw up heavily.

That was at age sixteen. She visited me just before her twenty-ninth birthday. She had married at twenty-six after a whirlwind romance with a man she had met three months earlier. She suffered having intercourse with him. It was the first time she permitted herself to have sex since the party ten year earlier. It was a dreadfully painful experience for her, but she had learned how to make the right noises. When he wanted to have anal sex she readily agreed, and it soon became their preferred way to have sex. She confessed that this way even brought her some pleasure – and that she didn't always have to act out that pleasure.

There was no sex at all after the marriage ceremony. At first she found what seemed to be appropriate excuses. After a while she didn't bother with any explanations. She told him to find a whore and that it wasn't going to be her. Three months after the wedding they had the marriage annulled.

Dorothy was a strikingly beautiful woman. It was my impression that her plastic surgeon had shaped her nose a fraction too narrow. She wore her high heels comfortably, and her rich platinum hair bounced just above her shoulders. Her dress, with its plunging neckline, was particularly daring with perhaps only a centimeter or two separating the edge of the material and her nipples. She worked at the reception desk of a major hotel – one of a large international chain – and was very adept at the practice of instant intimacy with the visitors to the hotel. They all loved her – even the women – and many told her how they regretted having to leave so soon and not having the chance to get to know her better. Dorothy had a collection of many dozens of business cards... "If you ever find yourself in my area..."

Dorothy, in fact, liked the company of men. She would seek long, deep, intimate discussions with them about feelings and needs. More often than not these men would feel that they were, in effect, being invited to progress to something more intimate and more physical with her, but at this point they would find her pulling away from them, instantly, coldly and without ceremony. She believed that having no need for any physical sexual intimacy was a natural condition. "I can't understand where there can be any real pleasure in copulation. It even looks dumb." She was convinced that most women let it happen only because they were afraid of finding themselves alone. This possibility never troubled her. She said she felt closer to her cat than to any man.

17. No One Listens. No One Hears.

L ibby, at twelve years old and in seventh grade, was a very outgoing and socially involved little girl. One day her mother approached her and told her that the shoes she was wearing were worn and probably too small, and that they would get her a new pair the following day.

Libby was so beside herself with joy that sleep didn't come until the early morning hours. She could see herself showing up at class in her new Adidas, Reeboks, Nike or whatever other super sport shoes, and the eyes of all her girlfriends would instantly pop out of their heads. Also, she was the last of her closest girlfriends to have great sport shoes. She never seriously pressed her parents for them because they were both hard working, and money in the family was scarce.

The next day was just as her mother had promised. They were just passing the store's display window when Libby saw the exact shoes she dreamed of. They were right smack there in the middle of all the other shoes. Overtaken with excitement and expectation, she literally bounced into the store pulling her mother behind her.

That excitement faded when after opening all the boxes

87

the clerk had set before them that shoe in the window was not there. She raced to the window display and pointed to the only shoe that mattered to her. Her mother tried to convince her that the other shoes were either nicer, or healthier, or more grown-up, or would last longer, but Libby's mood plummeted. From the tone of her mother's voice she knew this was not going to be a good day for her.

The clerk asked her to at least try on one pair to be sure of the exact size. In the end they left the store with a new pair of shoes, leaving behind the only pair that would surely have changed her life. She couldn't forgive her mother. At home her mother tried to soften her anger and mitigate her disappointment.

"Just try on the shoes. You'll see you'll like them. And believe me they are much healthier than the ones you wanted."

To no avail. Libby cried, "No one ever listens. No one ever hears. You can throw them in the garbage for all I care."

This was not an isolated incident. The experience of no one listening and no one hearing may come about any number of ways. Imagine a family watching television. The father, wanting to give some playful attention to his daughter sitting next to him, tickles her. She quietly asks him to stop. But it has become a kind of game for him. So he tickles her again, this time smiling mischievously. With this she turns to him in obvious annoyance and shouts for him to stop. But he persists, laughing loudly and enjoying himself immensely. The daughter is now more than annoyed. She is angry and short-tempered. She gets to her feet and goes to another part of the room. But he follows her... a great game for him, being comfortable with the fact that he is sharing an amusing moment with his daughter. She bursts angrily out the room, raging, exasperated, and close to tears. He doesn't listen. He doesn't hear.

Same thing when it came to buying a toy for a child. It would always be cheaper, smaller, and did fewer things than the toy the child dreamed of having. The child had repeated again and again, for weeks on end, exactly which toy he or she needed to have so badly. Again, no one listened. No one heard. No one never did. From the time Libby was well into her teens she avoided sharing anything of herself with her parents. That came, eventually, to include even her closest friends, which decidedly weakened the bonds between them. When she married her husband often complained how much of a stranger she remained to him – even in bed. Libby professed to have no idea why he should feel that way.

18. Madness as Greatness Misunderstood

Joshua was a man in his early forties when I met him. Born to a mother who had no idea who his father was, he had left his home and upbringing (such as it was) at the age of sixteen and joined the ranks of an ultra-orthodox religious sect that identified with cabbalistic magic and miracles. They had their mystical chants and fixed rituals, and for a time he knew a genuine joy in their company, and perfect happiness in his singular communion with God. This communion with God included many nights alone in secluded woods, along with extended periods of fasting. His feeling was that the closer he would come to the death of his body, the closer he would come to a truer and more authentic level of existence. He spoke of his mind at that time being flooded with the images of every manner of saint and sinner, of terrible devils and satyrs with cloven hooves, of violent winds and torrential rains. These images never left him and as much as he feared them he was obsessed with them, and they worked themselves deeply into the weave of his communication with himself.

At some point, in a frenzy, he began to slam his head against a wall. He came away from that wall not as Joshua but as Eliahu (Elijah). In his mind, Joshua, as a fornicating secular Jew, was doomed to burn forever in the fires of Purgatory. Joshua was without a license to life. Eliahu, who would henceforth devote himself to being God's messenger, would see to Joshua's demise.

Years went by. One day, as Eliahu, he passed an art supply shop and on impulse entered it. He was about twenty-four or twenty-five at the time. Half an hour later he emerged with an assortment of paints, brushes, oils, sketch pads and canvas sheets. His small one-and-a-half room flat on the ground floor of a somewhat rundown apartment complex led onto a balcony that the previous owner had closed in completely with ceiling-high plastic slat screens. The balcony became his studio.

It also became his universe. His visits to the woods became fewer and fewer until they stopped completely. At the same time the fervor of his religious devotion and his cries to God reached a pinnacle of sorts. When he described this period in his life, he said he felt at most as an unclean resident in his weak and emaciated physical body. His life, he said, where he lived and breathed and sang and danced was at an enormous distance from that body – in fact an entire planet removed from that body. He painted in a fury with the colors and the brushes more commanding him than he them. When the balcony could no longer contain all his works, he found an old carpenter's shed in the town and arranged to keep them there. He was alive and aflame.

Unfortunately, not for very long. A marriage was arranged by the movers and shakers of the sect with which he identified, and he met his wife (for the first time) under the ceremonial canopy. She was almost fifteen years his senior, divorced with four children. They all moved into that one-and-a-half room flat. He had to relinquish the balcony, and when his new wife took in his works for the first time she became hysterical and insisted that their marriage be annulled. With the intervention of the sect's elders, it was decided that the marriage would remain intact and that Eliahu would have to repent for sinking to the depths where only Satan reigned. There would be no more painting after that. He collected all his works and wrapped them in layers of paper and cloth. He placed them on the floor of the shed's upper level and made a pallet for himself on the bottom floor. He spent the next twelve years there, mostly in darkness, venturing out only rarely. His wife would bring him food and cigarettes, and after a time even these encounters with her passed in silence. Joshua, always trembling and terrified, would now surface in his mind with increasing frequency.

One day a newspaper article that carried my picture caught his eye. He had to read the lines through the food stains that had accumulated when his wife used the paper to wrap the food she brought him. We met a few days later. He had traveled almost two hundred miles to reach me bringing some of his sketch books and a few paintings on rolled-up canvases. Tears streamed from his eyes when he handed them to me.

They were incredible! I have no pretensions as a maven or art critic, but these were works unlike anything I had ever seen before. There was an intense fire raging in these paintings. Broad strokes of reds, oranges, greens, blacks and yellows delivered unapologetic images of men as beasts and beasts as men – all born on storms of lust with the most impossible configurations of sexual coupling stretching from one end of the canvas to the other. Here was no ordinary talent. The contortions of his mind, hammered by a history that included an alcoholic, part-time prostitute, and drug-addicted mother, punishing degradation at school for being born out of wedlock, and the terrors of abandonment when sent off at the age of eight to boarding school, at last found its voice in those brushes, paints and canvases.

This man was born with talents that translated as genius. He demonstrated a capacity for passion that carried him a remarkable distance when responsible only to himself. This distance may have been significant but it had the lifetime of a firefly. I try to think what heights of accomplishment he might have reached had the original "keyhole" – the home and life he was born into – been healthier, more accommodating, and altogether more in symmetry with what he had brought with himself when delivered into the world.

At the time of this writing it is almost twenty years since our meeting. I had learned (from his wife) that when Joshua would surface he would almost invariably seek refuge in a psychiatric hospital to escape the unforgiving ambitions of Eliahu. I don't know where Joshua, or Eliahu, is today or under what circumstances he is living. But I do know that he never returned to his brushes, oils and canvases. He (as Joshua) had promised solemnly that if that day ever came he would leave his first works on my doorstep. I believed him then and still do. When I open my front door each morning I look for them still. And taking a cue from Scarlet O'Hara I say to myself that tomorrow is another day.

19. Cellophane Man

When Steven was thirteen years old his uncle passed away and not long afterwards his mother brought home her brother's large record collection. Most of the records were LPs of works by Bach, Mozart, and Tchaikovsky. But looking through them, merely out of mild curiosity, and with no expectations, he came upon a small 45 Extended Play called Drumology. He played it and very soon found himself overtaken by a massive wave of excitement. It was a 45 of drum solos by Buddy Rich, Gene Krupa, Louis Bellson and Zutty Singleton. Steven decided there and then that he would be a drummer and that this would be his life.

Two years later he was good enough to be part of a small high school band. In his freshman year at university he was invited to join a combo that played at small clubs and cocktail lounges. In his sophomore year he backed singers cutting demos in sound studios.

He completed university with a BA. By this time the drums had lost much of their attraction for him, explaining that it involved having to share most of his time with other musicians, most of whom he felt were decidedly unhealthy. A more accurate explanation, but one left unsaid, probably had to do with a scary bout of syphilis that he got from one of the many girls who always seemed to shadow the musicians. But he also thought that his talent with the drums had peaked. Penicillin got him past the syphilis, but he couldn't get past the sense of emptiness that he now felt with his life as a drummer.

Along with a close friend from university, Steven opened a boutique coffee bar. The boutique style permitted a minimal investment, with old early movie posters serving as wallpaper and ceiling cover. Hard kitchen chairs, with wooden boxes on short legs for tables, were painted in every which color. There were low-set shelves of books and magazines. A pedal-driven Singer sewing machine, a vintage gramophone, and a heavy, antique, Atwater-Kent console radio contributed to the ambiance. Their most expensive acquisition, after the refrigerated counter, was the espresso machine that included a week in Milan learning about the preparation of espresso, cappuccino, and the more esoteric coffees that were fast becoming popular at the time.

It started off well. For a few months it was very much an "in" place, mainly with the crowd that still saw Steven as a class drummer. It was often frequented by musicians, old classmates, unpublished writers, rebellious, if unrefined, intellectuals whose conversations sparked loud philosophical and political discussions at almost all the other tables, and, surprisingly enough, a very civilized black-leather-jacketed motorcycle crowd.

After a while Steven found his enthusiasm for his coffee house waning. He frequently compared his obligations to his work as a Catholic marriage. There was no escaping the need to rise at seven each morning and make it to the baker's for the croissants, the Danish, and the cakes and pies. By eight the pressure in the espresso machine had to be high enough to accommodate the first orders. Just about every other morning he also needed a full half hour to clean and fine-tune the machine. And patrons were demanding that they stay open until after two in the morning. The money was good, but in the middle of their second year, Steven sold his share to his partner. His major complaint was that the work had taken over his life, which wouldn't have been so bad had it not also left him feeling so vacant and empty.

Steven's next move was to use a large bank loan to buy the building that housed the coffee shop. Using that building as collateral, he was able to buy another building, and then a third. His income now permitted the purchase of a comfortable five room house in a fashionable neighborhood. He was very close to proposing marriage to several of the women he had been dating. But that didn't happen. He would complain that he could not know who he really was to these women. How could they possibly find a place in his life, he thought, when he himself did not know where his place was in his own life. He moved into his new home still a bachelor at the age of thirty.

He was in his early fifties when I met him. Eventually he did marry, only to divorce after three years. He complained that the marriage had left him feeling empty. It added nothing to his life except a child. Even the advent of that child, now a teenager and an accomplished drummer in his own right, changed nothing.

His real estate ventures expanded and he became quite wealthy. For a time he fell in with a group that lived in the shadow of an Indian mystic and guru who established a large center in the Catskill Mountains. The mystic's own physical frailty, along with his penchant for fast cars and adoring women, struck Steven as being in perfect contradiction to the man's inspired words and visions. The day soon came when he turned his back on the guru and abandoned the group, leaving behind almost twenty thousand dollars.

In the wake of this experience he was interviewed for an article that appeared in a widely read daily newspaper. This caught the attention of a special interest group that invited him to speak to their members. At first he agreed, but a week before the date they had set he cancelled his appearance. His excuse was pressing affairs. The reason, in fact, was the terror he was experiencing at the prospect of standing before, and speaking to, an audience of strangers.

"Would you believe me if I told you that I felt I would stand there and have nothing to say? I really felt that they would look at where I was standing and find there was no one there. "And," almost speaking to himself, "why would anybody want to listen to me anyway?"

When we first met, Steven had shared with me a traumatic experience he had had as an eight year old boy that forever kept surfacing behind his eyes. His parents had taken him to a popular ocean beach when, for whatever reason, his mother had to rush home. Later his father had left for home thinking that Steven was with his mother. It was only very late that same evening when they realized that he had been left behind at the beach. Just as they were calling the police, the police appeared at their door with a weeping and trembling Steven in tow.

20. The Retreat to Paradise

Cheryl's life was the stage. She got her start at her university's theater group and from there to small roles in repertory theater. Other companies gave her work, and she was often sought out for important roles. There was never a critic's review that did not include accolades. She said that when handed a script and skimming through it for the first time she would instantly find herself in the skin and sharing the same mindset as the character she was to portray.

Cheryl married and had two children. Her husband adored her as she did him. She nursed each child for eight months and with both of them was prepared to continue for another eight months. Her career was on hold at this time, but she would say that what her children had added to her life more than compensated for whatever she left behind.

She described her life as a frightened child suffering from tics at her lips and her eyes – something that seemed to amuse other children but that her parents hardly noticed. The family unit consisted of her father, an auto mechanic, his loud, unemployed alcoholic brother, her depression-prone mother, and two older sisters. The eldest was diagnosed as autistic, although she wondered how that could be when they skipped rope and played hopscotch together. The second was diagnosed as suffering minimal brain damage because she was always failing at school. With so much going by so many people at such intense emotional levels, she found herself largely ignored, if not altogether forgotten.

She was still a few years short of her teens when she discovered how simple it was to shut herself out this world and let her unfettered imagination carry her to vistas deep within herself – to a paradise of fantasies. Here she soon found her natural and most inviting home. But for this to happen Cheryl had first to deflect any attention to herself. If she became the focus of the interest, concern or the demands of others, this gravitation to the refuge her inner world provided, would, necessarily, have been limited to her moments alone in bed before falling sleep. But she needed to return there often throughout the day. This was the only true sanctuary she had available to her. It was much too precious and inviting to forego even for a moment.

Herein, she felt, was the danger to herself - something which could very well happen were others to become knowledgeable of her secret. So to make herself virtually invisible to others she learned how to blend in with her surroundings by both flowing smoothly and perfectly with the moods and temper of the people around her. She also knew how to bury anything of herself that might suggest an ego. Assuming the nature of a chameleon was now not difficult for her. In fact, much like with the chameleon, it became virtually an instinctive reflex action.

She visited me because of a recurring dream that would have her awaken in the dead of night bathed in a cold sweat. She would be driving alone along an unfamiliar highway going faster than she liked. At a sharp curve in the road, she would lose control of the car, which would instantly careen off the road and plummet down a steep gorge. There was no escape and there was nothing to stop the fall of the car.

We linked that dream to her circumstances as a child where she had no reply to the life she had at home. As an adult, she could understand that that home had been completely dysfunctional, and that it had offered the child little more than a bed to sleep on and a roof over her head. Love, affection, a sense of containment, a sense of belonging and the experience of attachment were entirely unknown quantities. But without these quantities, and suffering the gross distortions in the roles her parents had assumed toward each other and toward the children, she was without any natural direction in her growth and development. In effect, her life was without any measure of coherence.

I suggested that perhaps before going to sleep she might again find refuge in that sanctuary of old... that "paradise of fantasies," or possibly return to it on awakening from the dream. She said my suggestion wouldn't be very helpful. "When the children were born," she said, "I never again found myself back with all those wonderful beings. More than I said good-bye to them, they said good-bye to me."

Eventually that dream left her and her nights were again peaceful. Not surprisingly, time again proved itself a great healer, with better tools and more adept at therapy than our most educated behavioral specialists. The only facet of Chery's last account of herself, and her life, that somewhat unsettled me (and continues to give me pause) was her confession that in bed with her husband, with their bodies firmly bonded, she would again feel herself outside her skin, back on center stage with the spotlight on her, hearing the applause of an adoring audience. She truly loved her husband, but in bed he could never be more than a supporting actor.

21. Dead on Arrival

Words maim. Words kill. Words bury. Sometimes, before the words are even understood the message received effectively undermines any genuine claim a person would have to his or her own life. This person's existence becomes bereft of any legitimacy. It is not a feeling that lends itself easily to translation into words. In the heart and mind of this person not a vestige of reason remains that may legitimize the space this person occupies on this planet. It is as though his or her body had somehow surfaced in this physical and material world yet had, in fact, been dead on arrival.

Jana was a girl who could cry and smile at the same time. She could share with me episodes in her childhood that had left the deepest scars – scars that probably would never heal. Yet with tears glistening on her cherubic cheeks, a shy trembling smile would play at her lips as though suggesting that, somehow, she knew that she too had a role in those ugly bits and pieces of her history.

Jana was twenty-six and in the process of breaking up with her boyfriend. They were living together for over a year and she had no problem admitting that he was totally devoted to her. In fact, that was the problem. He was a very caring, quiet, generous, serious, intelligent person, and successful as a certified chartered public accountant. He was almost eleven years older than her. Perhaps because of his age, she thought, it was his oft-repeated wish that they marry and start a family. There was nothing she could say about him that even hinted of complaint. There was no other man in her life. And, truthfully, there was no other man that she wanted in her life. Yet she knew he was right whenever he accused her of her turning her back on him. That wasn't what she wanted to believe, but she knew in her heart what he was feeling.

Her only explanation was that she was blind and stupid. It was what both her parents had repeatedly told her, and of course they were right. It was also about the only common ground she could remember that her forever-warring parents had ever shared.

To make matters worse, she had stopped working and had no idea how she would cover the rent in the coming months. She had a degree in computer programming, and over the four years that she worked at a bustling hi-tech firm had been awarded two significant promotions with the way open to more. But she was never sure in her heart that this was where her life should be. She was convinced that she missed out by not going to acting school.

The same questions surfaced with regard to her boyfriend. Perhaps if she had been spared having to forever tend to her long-suffering mother and suffer the foul mouth and violent behavior of her father, she might have had a healthier bearing on the course of her own life. In her heart, however, she knew where to find the answers. It was as though having come into the world by sheer accident, unwanted and uninvited, her entire existence was bereft of legitimacy. When she would turn her back to her boyfriend and deny him his pleasures it was the only way she had to tell him not to attach his life to one who had no claim to any legitimate place in this world.

"I was an accident," she said. "In my entire life I could never imagine them coming together to bring a child into the world. And if I had a dime for all the times my mother told me how she wished for an abortion when she learned she was pregnant with me, I'd be owning a condominium today."

22. Finding His Mother

As a child, Jerome always suffered his mother's ridicule. She forever compared him to her useless failure of a husband – and in general belittled him for having been born a male. She punished him by denying him the chocolate cookies and cakes he so loved, and more than once locked him in a dark closet for half an hour if he did something that displeased her. And yet, she had breastfed him for a full eight months, and had no objection to keeping him in her bed where he could continue to absorb the warmth and smells of her body and her marvelous physical presence. When he was four or five years old, his parents divorced and she became a very angry, bitter and punishing woman. This wasn't the mother he once knew. But oddly enough, he found that if he became ill, or got hurt, that original, concerned and caring angelic mother might instantly reappear. These instances were rare but never forgotten.

As an adult Jerome became very successful and very rich in real estate dealings. He had a degree in law but no desire to practice it. His businesses expanded to include importing textiles and furniture. He also had significant holdings in oil companies, restaurants and hotels. Once a week Jerome, in his chauffeured limo, visited a middle aged woman who would have him undress, suck on her toes and later, with him in the bathtub, urinate all over his back. While on all fours she would make him bark like a dog and lick her legs. If he let up for a moment she whipped him. With each visit she devised some new demeaning punishment that he "deserved" *for being a bad boy.* In the end he would weep bitterly. After a moment alone, the woman would embrace him warmly, kiss his cheek and wipe away the tears. Each visit lasted for about an hour and each time he left one thousand dollars on her dresser.

It was the only way he knew how to reach his mother.

Jerome never married.

23. The Chemistry of Same Sex Relationships

Let me say at the very outset that a good number of homosexuals have contributed enormously to my professional career, and the realization of my very personal existentialist ambitions. The words have not yet been invented that can describe how grateful I shall forever be to a number of them. However, if the practice may be visualized in the context of the somewhat flippant title *Dead-End Sex*, I would attempt to describe a very specific etiology of homosexuality, using the term as an umbrella to cover both men and women.

This will take some explaining, but I'll say at the outset that what I will attempt to deliver to the reader is merely some understanding how homosexuality, as a program of sexual identification, via the vehicles of learning and conditioning, may overtake a personality essentially free of genetic determinants. When its specific expressions originate in the very early home environment, the chemistries manifest here are probably more rife and touches more lives than does any other explanation, including organic, for this sexual style and practice.

There would be many instances where homosexuality is, indeed, an extension of genetic configurations. There is nothing to explain or debate here, and nothing to be apologetic about when homosexuality is a genetically determined quantity. Indeed one can only understand the anguish of those finding themselves in bodies unrelated to the experience of their sexual identification. Nevertheless, given the conditions that envelope the planet with life, there has to be something decidedly malevolent in a genetic configuration programmed, essentially, to self-destruct. An individual's genetic makeup is, after all, a closed-circuit arrangement. It would not be alert to the fact that there are other people who can, and would, procreate. But contributing to the continued survival of any population is not in the program of their biology, or an interest central to their concerns.

Then there are instances of homosexuality where people, mostly young, permit themselves be influenced by the juggernaut of gay propaganda, as if by not being partner to the gay experience they will somehow be missing out on a wonderful life experience. With so many great and attractive people coming out of their proverbial closets, and with all those marvelous parades and parties and ready partners, they see this community as the "in" crowd and the "now" people.

Then there is an identification with a homosexual lifestyle that originates with an absent father – absent in the sense that he is largely physically absent or a grey figure in the background. The mother dominates. She is the omnipresent definer of the temper and character of the household. It is from here that these lines will carry.

If we understand the components of the neonate's global auto-erotic experiences with the mother's body, we will then understand developments here. The infant came into the world and was deposited in its mother's arms. Its lips found the nipple and its head became cushioned in the mother's breast. Warm milk was delivered to its mouth and from there to its belly. The warmth and smells of the mother's body rise up to completely envelop the child. There is the sound of her voice, the beating of her heart, and the gentle shifting of her body. All this creates an idyllic environment wherein the child, still a neonate, enjoys a sense of security, a sense of completion and total well-being. Part of the same wondrous package of the neonate's experiences include its own natural bodily functions including, the simple and possibly pleasurable experience of its excretory organs.

These experiences are labeled *auto-erotic* because without any knowledge of the mother as a body external to its own, they touch and envelop the infant as though originating with its own body. It will take some time before the infant gets to recognize the mother as the true source of its sensory pleasures. Meanwhile the infant's own body is experienced as the source of all that knows such marvelous sense of bonding and containment.

As the child begins to develop its motor and cognitive faculties and discovers that there is a new and marvelous dimension external to the mother experience, it is absolutely vital at this time that the father has a strong presence in its life. Consider that the infant comes upon the father, again in a dimension very much external to its early virtually organic mother absorption experiences, in a dimension that extends from the father and that now includes everyone else. When the infant, male or female (makes no difference), enjoys a true attachment to, and identification with, a full father-experience, it is this collective, all-encompassing experience that becomes the filter through which the child accesses and finds a place in the larger and more distant social world. The father, as the infant's first link to the world external to itself, becomes its surest bridge to this new dimension.

The package that is the father-experience pretty near duplicates the experience of identification, attachment and bonding that the child had originally known with its mother. The child recognizes and introjects the experience of the father's identifying with it, becoming the focus of his attentions, along with the very physical experience of being held and carried by him. The package, in fact, includes just about everything the infant had known with its mother with one very important and very critical exception; *it does not include the auto-erotic body experiences.*

What the reader may come to understand is that it is specifically this arrangement that assures that almost everybody in this world is born heterosexual (excepting, of course, where genetic factors, or otherwise inherited factors, override the natural chemistries initiated by this father-experience – and these numbers may be considerable). The vastly expanded number of those identifying with a homosexual lifestyle is created when it is not the father who serves as the infant's bridge to the larger world of people, but the mother and the rich auto-erotic experiences... the rich and so very intimate body experiences that she alone was responsible for.

This progression to an expanded external world consciousness does not wait for the father, or for the essential father-experiences noted earlier. If the father isn't there, it will be the mother and the mother-experience that delivers the child to this new world dimension. Specifically, it would be through the filter of the rich mother-experience that the child will effect its connection to the social world. And the manner in which we described the father-experience serving as the infant's bridge to its social world, so may we expect it to be perfectly duplicated by the mother-experience. Admittedly, a loving, containing and emotionally bonded mother will equally promise that the infant will get to merge comfortably and fluidly with the mainstream of all social groupings it will identify with in the future.

As the years pass childhood gives way to adolescence and then adulthood. The biological and hormonal changes which are now a function of this progression to adulthood begin to create heightened needs and drives of a decidedly sexual nature. What remains is for these needs and drives to be given direction.

When it is the mother-experience that serves as the filter through which the child accesses and communicates with the other-people world, we have the original auto-erotic experiences coming into very powerful play. Inasmuch as they stem from the infant's earliest pre-conscious experiences they continue to have a critical hold on its mind. There will be something decidedly deterministic about their imprint on that individual's identification with himself, or herself... virtually dictating the natural targets of those needs and drives.

What develops at this time could never have come about had the child its father-experiences to effect that bridge. When the individual has only the temper of his, or her, earliest mother-experiences, each will recall and be powerfully moved to seek and re-experience the original, all encompassing, and totally gratifying auto-erotic experiences – *essentially the experience of his, or her, own sexual organs along with other own-body experiences.* Make no mistake, the excitement is very real and very intense. Right here you have the inexorable gravitation to homosexual styles and practices that are experienced as entirely organic phenomenon. It becomes a virtually organic development, and, again, applies equally to both sexes.

Here, more explicitly, is the crunch. In a social environment these people may come upon others of the same sex, and with that single encounter feel themselves overtaken by a tension they can neither break nor entirely understand. It is a tension that, as just noted, has deep roots in those very early auto-erotic experiences with their own sexual and sensory organs – experiences hidden from conscious memory, but not from the body's core-identity memory. These bring this person to somehow sense that through that other person's body, *as a physical projection of his, or her, own,* he, or she, may somehow relive those powerful, emotionally charged, utterly magical, and altogether sublime pleasures that his, or her, own body had apparently never forgotten.

Sometimes the father-experience is there but in a relatively weak format – something somewhat vague and vacant of the indelible markings true of the mother-experience. With all that concerns the filter through which the infant accesses its social world, it cannot overtake the mother-experience with its rich and powerful auto-erotic constituents. In such instances the father-experience may become manifest as a variable – sometimes weaker sometimes stronger. Given this spectrum with its range of possibilities the individual may demonstrate bisexual behaviors.

At the risk of upsetting the temper of the subject as presented here, there may be room to demonstrate, somewhat crudely perhaps, that those early, own-body, experiences are never forgotten by anyone at any time. If apologies will be in order I will offer them now. But consider the gross unpleasantness verging on disgust when in a room heavy with the flatulence of another person. Yet the experience in the nostrils of the flatulence issued by one's own body is actually quite pleasurable – even having a calming effect. It links the mind and the memory with the security that came with that original organic bonding. With this behind us, (no pun intended,) we'll move on.

24. The Paranoia of a Piranha

Over the phone he made an appointment in the name of Rob. I thought the name was somewhat apt as he proved to be an officer in the police force, originally with the fraud squad, now with the rank of Police Detective. This had put him in the front ranks of those investigating homicides, grand larceny, kidnappings and increasingly, among other unsavory practices, slavery.

Rob was a huge specimen of a man. He was out of uniform when I met him, but I could imagine how, when in uniform, merely his shadow would suffice to intimidate and bring to a tremble anyone with a bad conscience. His hands might have been mistaken for baseball mitts, but apart from their extraordinary size the skin at the back of his hands seemed as smooth, as clear, and as white as a baby's bottom.

I soon understood that he came, and was prepared to pay for the cost of the session, only to get a look at me. He had learned that his girlfriend, who was also with the police and dealing mostly with instances of child molestation, had visited me a week ago. What concerned him was what issues she presented and what we had spoken about. Before I could tell him that there were laws protecting the confidentiality of our meeting, he started in to tell me of a visit he paid to her gynecologist.

"There are good women gynecologists but she had to open her legs to a man. So I broke his legs. Both of them."

It crossed my mind that perhaps my own legs would soon be in disrepair, but I believed he saw me as a tepid endomorph, and no great prize to any woman. His eyes had lost their piercing penetration of my own. If a mesomorph is the muscular athletic type with broad shoulders and a narrow waist, the endomorph is built exactly the same way only the other way around.

"So what did she have to say for herself?"

"If I so much as started to tell you, you would have to arrest me. It was all of one session and it would be her decision to decide what to share with you. I'm not going to lose my license over something that's nothing." On reflection I thought that he might find the information he was looking for in that last line – inasmuch as the syntax was definitely wanting.

Still, he was fishing. "I don't trust her, doctor. She looks innocent but I'm sure she's seeing men. I don't trust her. She's hiding things from me."

"You shouldn't have broken his legs."

"He should be thankful I didn't take his eyes out."

"But what makes you so certain that she is not being faithful to you? I think you are going overboard and being a little paranoid."

"PARANOID???!!! LIKE BEING CRAZY IN THE HEAD???"

"Paranoid isn't crazy," I ventured, trying to elevate myself to a professional academic level. "If you were crazy you would never be in the responsible position you have with the police force. (*Patronizing him slightly couldn't hurt*). Being paranoid means that you would take as fact what you merely suspect – not what you know, or what you can prove."

"Let me add to your education, doctor" he said in the sort of hushed voice that, at least in Hollywood, comes an instant before a fist smashes into a face. "I'm recognized as the best on the force because of this nose", he said, pointing at it. "I got promoted twice because I'm the best at my job. Don't call me sick in the head."

"I can well believe that. And I didn't say you were sick *anywhere*." That, at least, was what I had said – as opposed to what I now knew with considerable certainty.

"And I know things. I got a girl on the force who I fuck now and then, to be my wife's best friend. And she tells me everything – like this visit to you."

"And the visit to the gynecologist."

"That too."

"What about being with other men?"

"That will come".

25. Itsy Bitsy Misty

Itsy bitsy, teeny weeny, yellow polka dot bikini…" This was the refrain Misty would hear often through public and high-school. She was the tiniest of the girls in her class, and more than once she heard herself being described by older folks as a miniature China doll.

Misty had been adopted when she was less than a month old so that her place in the family had her feel entirely as an organic extension of both parents. The fact of her adoption was never hidden from her. She was in her late teens when she learned that her biological mother had given birth to her at the age of 15.

In her years at high school her friends took to calling her "Itsy" and Misty had no objections – or at least none that she had ever voiced. If some of her friends were known familiarly as "Scratchy" and "Loosely" and "Jan-Jan", the names all carried a message of belonging and acceptance.

She remembered her high school days as deliriously fun days. Because of her diminutive size and athleticism she became a prominent member of a competitive cheerleading squad. She would be thrown high in the air and somersault forwards and backwards, landing on her feet on the hands of the stronger boys. She thought it was really sexy to wear those tight red underpants under a very short skirt and showing it all when doing the splits in the air. The team never made better than 3rd place in the competitions, but that never mattered to her.

At university she had her name back, and with it some serious attention from sophomores and seniors. Her figure filled out in a manner that had her backside recall the popular 18th century fashionable padding the ladies liked there, and she knew which sweaters and blouses showed her breasts at their most inviting. More than one lecturer found it difficult to have his eyes leave her.

She studied Criminology seeing herself in the not too distant future as a probation officer. Her courses included lectures on the behavioral sciences and social work, and her grades were consistently high. Between semesters and papers that needed writing she traveled to Paris and Madrid. Another time it was London. In her first meaningful relationship she travelled with her partner, an architect, and a wine *aficionado*, to Tuscany, visiting some popular wineries. They walked through rows of grape vines, sampled the marvelous Tuscan Chianti wines, met the warmest people, and were literally feted at the many family trattorias dotting the countryside. He was also a wonderful partner in the beds they shared.

Misty was certain they would eventually marry, but when he fell victim to what the doctors called ocular hypertension that might lead to glaucoma, threatening to impair both his vision and his career, she drifted away. She never lacked suitors, and those she liked she tested, almost unmercifully, their professed loyalty to her. They invariably failed.

Her professors thought she might do well continuing to a master's degree in criminology but Misty no longer identified with the labors of a probation officer. She felt a particular aversion to the impoverished, unstable and entirely unclean environments that she would have been obliged to visit and revisit. There was that, and the ever-present threat of violence when twisted minds and tempers made predicting what she would encounter there quite impossible. This wasn't her "scene" as she put it.

Her parents doted on her every way they could. They were financially well off and were genuinely pleased to share as much as they could with her. Among other things it translated into an expensive BMW 2 seater and fashionable clothes. At the same time Misty seemed, ever so innocently, to test even their loyalty by willfully disappointing them when she could – mostly by not returning their calls. They always "understood."

Misty found work as a spokeswoman for a national political party, and it was here that she met Amos, an effusive, charming lawyer who was a lobbyist for the local offices of that party. He had the whitest teeth and flawless, professionally manicured nails. He also had a strong chin and dimpled cheeks when he smiled – which was always – so he found no advantage in stylish and trimmed facial hair. Misty and Amos were frequently obliged to work together and fix on strategies. They seemed always to be of one mind with the ideas of one fueling the creative talents of the other.

Their wedding made the social pages in several newspapers. Many hundreds of guests arrived. Their numbers included the famous in the entertainment industry, sports personalities, the politically promising – and those simpler folk on Misty's side. It mattered not. They were happy for her, and happy that they could see her now so beautiful, so healthy, so grown up, so adored by all, and plainly so financially secure.

Andrew was Amos's best friend from their high school days. Married to Cynthia – a creative fashion designer – they became an inseparable foursome. Andrew owned a fine, 2 bedroom and very seaworthy yacht. Around their first wedding anniversary Amos suggested that they all fly to some Greek island. Andrew had a better idea. He hired three licensed skippers to bring his yacht to a marina on the French Riviera, and from there he took over the wheel, sailing them to ports from Herzliah (Tel-Aviv), to Antalya on the Turkish Riviera, through several Greek islands, to the castled city of Dubrovnik. The three licensed skippers were flown to Dubrovnik, given the yacht to bring home, while the foursome made the return trip in the first class of an Alitalia jet.

While in Dubrovnik, with Amos and Cynthia out shopping and scouting for good restaurants, Misty got into bed with Andrew.

No one was ever the wiser. The four would always be together. There was tennis, bridge, club shows, private screenings, restaurants, and horse racing with their camaraderie marvelously and perfectly entrenched. At the same time Misty and Andrew seemed always able to find an hour or two when they could have time together alone. They had their trysts about once every week or two, and they carried on this way for more than four years, never arousing the slightest hint of suspicion.

The marriage between Amos and Misty ended when Amos confessed one evening that he had been seeing another woman. It was his decision to tell Misty because that woman threatened to do so herself if Amos failed to pay her a generous sum of money to win her silence.

Misty became uncontrollably hysterical. Aiming for his eyes her scratches brought blood streaking down the sides of his face. "You abandoned me" she shrieked at him, "like my fucking mother abandoned me." She smashed a Doha Chinese porcelain vase and ripped a portrait of herself out of its frame on the wall. With that she removed all her clothes, and rushed out into the night. Amos couldn't catch up to her but a motorist called the police who soon found her. They had an ambulance collect her and the medics struggled to strap her to the bed. Amos tried speaking to her quietly as the ambulance made its way to the hospital emergency ward. Misty continued shrieking about her mother abandoning her. The medics attempted to stem the bleeding from Misty's scratches but Amos pushed them away.

An injection brought calm and exhaustion brought sleep. Misty was diagnosed as having had an acute schizophrenic episode, which, if it persists in spite of the drugs she would be given, would require her condition to be reassessed at a later date.

26. Do What Daddy Tells You

When Simon saw his daughter for the first time in the hands of the nurse in the maternity ward he would have sworn that at no time in his life had he known such complete… such perfect happiness. It didn't matter that her face seemed overly red and somewhat swollen over one eye, the nurse was smiling and fingering a curl when she asked him whether in his life he had ever seen something so beautiful.

Simon recalled the night of her conception. Rose had been on the pill from the time they started sleeping together, but into their second year of marriage they had switched to condoms to give Rose's biology a chance to regain its balance. Then came the night when they decided to go for a baby. Simon recalled that his excitement had pitched higher, with his heart beating faster than ever. He could even hear the pounding of his heart inside his ears. They looked into each other's eyes as though seeking reassurance that both knew that this was it. Simon then ejaculated longer, his body overtaken by more powerful, uncontrollable spasms than he had ever, in the 26 years of his life, experienced. He didn't have to wait to learn that Rose had missed her period. He knew from that moment that there was a baby inside her.

127

Debbie enriched his life no end. Before she walked she learned how to bounce on the springs of her jumpchair, and in it she would reach wherever on the floor she wanted to be. He would read her picture stories, and watch her pound with delight on the xylophone bars. When out for walks she would be perched on his shoulders, or else watching the world from her stroller.

When in kindergarten he would ask her what she did, who her best friends were, and did she learn a new song. In her room he had cards with all the letters of the alphabet tacked in their order, in a row, close to the ceiling. With a stick for a pointer he would point to each letter in turn while singing the ABC song. At the PQRS he would suddenly open his eyes as wide as he could, then, an instant later, bend down and tickle her. Knowing it was coming she would start giggling the moment he started the song. In his heart he felt that if anything "bad" was ever to happen to her, his life would be over.

In grades one and two Debbie would share with him what they were learning and what chores the teacher had given them. These chores were mostly drawing pictures of the stories they were reading. Simon would watch with great interest what images Debbie would deliver to her drawing book. He would be effusive with his praise but almost invariably had suggestions how her drawings could be improved.

In her later years at public school he would show enormous interest in how she related to the other children – and how they related to her. There were times when he expressed a dislike of a certain child, perhaps because of something he knew of that child's parents, and he would caution Debbie not to get too friendly with her. This was also the first time Debbie heard the line: "Listen darling (or listen sweetness) I'm a little older than you. I have more experience than you. I know a little better than you. Do what daddy tells you and you will always be doing the right thing." It was a line repeated in any number of variations throughout all her years at school.

When Debbie reached Junior High Simon shared with her his thoughts and opinions on just about every issue that mattered – issues related to interactions with teachers, homework assignments, closest friends, appropriate clothes, extracurricular activities, day trips, and especially boys. He always knew what was best to believe, to say, to reply, and to initiate. He always knew how best to react in any given situation, and the importance of always making good impressions.

On more than one occasion Debbie's mother tried explaining to Simon that the nature of his affection for the girl was not helpful at all for her growth and development. She tried to have him understand that a child has to learn from personal experience. Her kindergarten experience is as important as a college education because here she gets her first lessons on how to interact with her peers. Everything in her years growing up is trial and error. If she is not going to fail at things, if she is not going to be disappointed when her expectations burst like balloons, how else will she ever learn the connection between what she wants and what efforts are needed to realize those wants. What Simon was doing, she insisted, was teaching Debbie that if she ever wanted to lift something that weighed a pound, in her daughter's mind a single ounce of effort should suffice. "And that won't work!" "All I'm doing" Simon would offer by way of reply, "is to spare her making mistakes. That's all."

Nothing changed. Simon thought that Debbie always demonstrated an analytical mind and a grasp of details. He thought that she would do well studying law. Her grades permitted acceptance in a respected law school and she identified comfortably with his suggestion.

A problem of another order arose when she developed a romantic interest in another law student. They met for coffee and another time took in a Chekov play. When he attempted to kiss her she seemed to be with him until at the last moment she turned her face away and his lips met her cheek. But she squeezed his hand saying she really liked him adding that she would feel a lot more comfortable if he took "these things" slowly.

Debbie exited the car feeling very angry with herself. How she reacted to him was plainly dumb. But why, if she genuinely wished for a relationship to develop between them would she deny something as innocent as a good-night kiss? The answer, she knew, was that she would soon be telling her father how their date went. He would want very much to know. He would also know if she was hiding something or being dishonest.

For this reason Debbie never permitted any suitor to bring his hand under her bra. She would never permit her own hand to touch her partner's penis, or have a man's hand reach under her panties. Oral sex was definitely out as was any other kind of sex.

Debbie left her law studies sometime during her first year of apprenticeship with a highly respected law firm. In any debate, or at any conference, in fact at any meeting that required discussion, it was always her conviction that anyone demonstrating authority surely knew more, and knew better, than she did. If ever she would be required to defend a client in court she knew her arguments would crumble in the wake of anyone speaking with authority opposing them.

When Simon protested her decision Debbie lashed at him madly and blindly. She accused him of ruining her life. So thick with uncontrolled and unrestrained anger and rage were the words that issued from her lips that a thin froth came to the sides of her mouth. It met the tears that flowed in a torrent from her eyes.

It wasn't long afterward that her parents divorced. Debbie married when she was nearing her forties, to a man, ten years her senior, divorced with four children. She worked as a librarian at a high school library.

27. "Look what you are always doing to me."

Her mother slaved for everyone. She would clean the house until dropping from exhaustion. There was always something on the stove and in the oven invariably accompanied by her loud complaints that everything was ruined because her father had failed to bring home the right this, or the right that, from the shopping list she had given him. The clothes she wore might have come off the back of a homeless and destitute refugee, and that the only things that mattered in her life were the children. Everything she did, she insisted, was for the children.

Beverly never doubted it, although somewhere behind her eyes, with the consistency of a faint, distant, ghostly apparition, were thoughts of a mother who was never there for her. She was the eldest of three children – herself and two younger brothers – and could remember the efforts she had made, even as a young child, to win her mother's attention and affection. A smile seemed to be an expression foreign to any of the arrangements her mother's thin lips and heavy eyes could ever manage.

Beverly learned to study her mother's moods, opinions and general mindset. She had a pretty fair idea what would surely provoke her and what might please her. With the start of each day she would measure the tone of her mother's voice taking careful note of whatever, at that hour, might be pressing on her mind. Guessing was never necessary as her mother, in both regards, kept nothing to herself. Outfitted with this knowledge Beverly was often able to effect some measure of control over her mother's attitude to her and how she would carry on relating to her.

There was the occasional slip up. She could remember as a five or six year old playing in a park sandbox, falling on a corner in a way that tore a trouser leg near the knee leaving a scratch that started to bleed. Wailing loudly, she rushed to her mother's side a short distance away. On seeing the rip, and quite impatient with her daughter's distress, her mother shouted at her.

"Look what you are doing to me. Look what you are ALWAYS doing to me."

With that, Beverly's attentions instantly became dislocated from the fright and the pain that had overtaken her, and again had her focus on what her mother was feeling.

Often she would hear her mother describe her to relatives and neighbors as a gift from heaven, so perfect, so considerate, so intelligent, so everything. But Beverly could never recall an intimate moment with her mother where the latter would translate those feeling into words meant specifically for her own ears.

Often her success with this defensive strategy came at a price. When she returned from her grade three class with her teacher's effusive compliments on her handwriting, her mother's eyes opened wide with something, truly nearing a smile, playing at her lips. Clearly she had made her mother happy. More important, she could feel that her mother was happy having her as her daughter. The experience was repeated several times in her early school years, so that, at least in this regard, Beverly linked her mother's acceptance with her bringing home the best grades.

If her mark on any high school examination fell below 100 her shame would induce a depression which had her lock herself in her room to cry hysterically into her pillow. On the rare occasion when a mark she received fell by so much as a single point below that of another pupil she wouldn't go home until one of her brothers would come to fetch her. Her anxiety and shame at such times would be so intense that ending her life became an inviting option. Even when her mother would try to tear her away from her books and papers, which always came at the expense of time outside with her friends, it was to no avail.

She resisted dating, and avoided parties. The one she went to with a date was a New Year's Eve party planned to extend until breakfast at a downtown restaurant the following morning. At one:ten her date had to bring her home. Beverly was ready to return home fifteen minutes after arriving at the party – after comparing the drab outfit she was wearing to the dazzling parade of chic and sexy outfits the other girls had on.

Having the best grades in her final year at high school Beverly was invited by the principal to address the pupils, their parents and guests at the graduation ceremony. Beverly felt her knees about to give way. The offer terrified her. She shook her head from side to side sharply enough for the principal to understand there was no point pressing her… that he would have to look elsewhere. At the same time Beverly was hugely pleased to have had this offer to share with her mother.

Beverly's first hint at the problems she would be encountering in the future came when she registered at university having no idea the direction her studies might take. She was equally as good at math as she was with literature. She had excelled at both history and biology. When she tried to think what she liked best her mind went blank. It crossed her mind that from childhood no communication had ever transpired between her and herself – that from the very first it had always been between herself and her mother.

In the end she opted for psychology and philosophy. Her commitment to either was painfully shallow. Equally shallow was her commitment to a romantic relationship.

At the age of nineteen she permitted herself the experience of sexual intercourse with a young man majoring in English literature. She was accommodating more her curiosity than any profound libidinal needs or drives. More than once it crossed her mind that her interest in men perfectly duplicated the interest her mother had had in her father.

Beverly graduated summa cum laude in her master's program in psychology. Clinical psychology held no attraction for her but she opted, nevertheless, to carry on to a doctoral program.

She married a chemistry professor whom she suspected had homosexual leanings. This quite suited her as his sexual interest in her largely duplicated her sexual interest in him. After their second year of marriage sex was a subject that was neither discussed nor ever again practiced. But a son had been born to them and Beverly felt wholly devoted to him. However it happened one day after a heavy rainfall that her son came home with his clothes, for whatever reason, soaked and muddied. Something in her spirit had snapped.

"Look what you are doing to me" she suddenly shouted at him. "Look what you are ALWAYS doing to me."

28. "I have you and you have me."

It crossed Jerry's mind that at the age of 68, with both parents deceased, as was surely true of all his public school teachers, there was no one alive who might remember his grade 5 folly of changing a few grades on his report card. His talent at this criminal enterprise was somewhat less than professional. As young as he was, he understood that he would be shamefully exposed, when it promised as well to bring the imprint of his father's five fingers down on his face and backside. Besides, with the ink having run, there was no way it could be returned in that condition to his class teacher. He cut the report card into shreds and deposited them in an alley dustbin.

Most of the week passed quietly until the class teacher finally grasped that Jerry would not be returning the report card signed or unsigned. A call to his parents brought them to the school where a thoroughly shamed and tearful Jerry suffered the unholy pummeling of their wrath on his head. Later that day at home his father completed this chapter in Jerry's upbringing with a particularly savage beating. The thought that came to him as he crouched in a corner of the kitchen waiting for the next blow, was why his mother was never ever there to stop the beating. At the same time, he was saying to himself that one day his father would be as feeble as his grandfather and would never dare raise a hand at him when that day would come.

When the beating was over Jerry's father tightened his lips over bared teeth and hissed: *"The difference between you and me is that I have you, and you have me."* Translated, he was saying that while Jerry had a respected, successful and wealthy dentist for a father who permitted the boy to live in a fine home, he himself had only this brainless, imbecilic son who would never amount to anything in his entire, miserable, parasitic life.

It was less than a year later that his father had lost a good deal of that respect. He was accused by several of his younger patients of sex offences including outright rape. He was tried, convicted and later sentenced to twenty years' incarceration at a state penitentiary. His practice was over, his license was revoked, and most of his wealth landed in the pockets of his lawyers. He was released after fourteen years and not once in all that time would Jerry accompany his mother on her visits to him.

Jerry had struggled through public school. He fared somewhat better in high school. There he played on the basketball team winning considerable popularity and not a little attention from the girls. After a year working at odd jobs he managed to find the means to pay for a university education. His mother had found work as a dress designer and her labors there were greatly appreciated. They were obliged to sell their home and accept something far less opulent in a poorer part of the city, but they managed to keep their heads above water owing nothing to anybody.

Jerry grew into a muscular heavyweight. His neck thickened and his broad, shoulders slanted into long powerful arms. Early in his freshman year the coach of the football team had been advised to seek him out and take the boy's measure as a potential player. Jerry had basketball more in mind but went along with the coach's invitation. They found that he was a particularly swift runner, could maneuver his body with the natural agility that he had gained from his time on the basketball courts, and had good hands for handling the ball. The single downside that the coach thought could be corrected was his inherent gentleness. Jerry was averse to hurting anyone.

Playing for the first time as a tight end Jerry fumbled the first ball thrown at him by a quarterback without options. He caught another pass for a first down but was brought down hard before he could get his legs under him. In the same game he was criticized for missing a crucial block for a running back. The coach thought Jerry would do better as a wide receiver and teamed him up in practice sessions with a second string quarterback and a pass interceptor.

In the next game against the team leading the league he caught three long passes for two touchdowns. The first was a single hand catch, well overthrown, but which Jerry somehow got to and had the ball bounce on his fingertips until he controlled it. This brought everyone in the stands to their feet.

At university he earned a degree in civil engineering but only got to work in the field fifteen years later. He had signed a contract with a moneyed club in the National Football League and soon saw his bank account swell to several million dollars. Action photographs of his catches emblazoned the sport pages and he couldn't walk in the street or sit in a restaurant without being recognized and photographed for perpetuity in selfies with smiling strangers.

His first serious love affair was with a young hotel housekeeper from Hong Kong who would clean his hotel room and prepare his bed. He thought she was more beautiful than any woman he had ever known in his life. He brought her to his home, bought her a fine car and gave her as much money as she asked for and then some. She showed remarkable talent with clothes and fashion styles and he purchased a small boutique for her in which he enlisted his mother to help her manage.

They were an excellent team working well together, and the boutique thrived.

Not so the relationship between them. After slightly more than a year Jerry found himself impossibly impotent when in bed with her. The same impotence never carried through with several other ladies, all discrete and lovely, that he had permitted himself to visit every now and then. It seriously unnerved him until he grasped the reason why. When, in silence, he looked at the girl, and listened to her soft breathing, something about her eyes, the sad turn of her lips, and her shy reticent manner, had him recall his mother. For a flickering moment he was once again the young boy crouching in the corner receiving his father's murderous blows, with his mother, standing nearby, not once rescuing him from that, or any other beating.

His father lived an empty life ever since his release. Ruptured aneurisms in his cortex eventually crippled him. In the rehabilitation hospital he would spend hours fitting plastic squares, circles and triangles into their pockets on a board. Jerry rarely visited him, but when he did he would sit at his father's side and say in a voice just above a whisper: *"The difference between you and me, Pa, is that I have you and you have me."* His father only smiled, understanding not a word. He was never forgiven. Not even at age 68 with his father having long ago been delivered to his grave.

29. God's Blessings

Bruce was born after 26 weeks gestation weighing 1 pound 8 ounces. He had spent close to four months in a neonatal care unit incubator connected to feeding and oxygen tubes with the doctors unable to assure his parents that he would survive his first day, let alone his first year. He was born before it became standard practice for the mother to sit by the incubator massaging him and exercising his arms and legs, so, in effect, Bruce was denied any early experience with human touch or warmth.

It had been a devastating experience for his parents, William and Sandra, both medical students aiming for careers in psychiatry. Something in their hearts and minds had switched off the issue of her womb. They spoke about feeling that he was as lost to them as they were to him, deciding it was safest not to bond emotionally to his being. Their visits became increasingly infrequent and they demonstrated no pleasure when told, one day, that he could go home with them.

Sandra's mother was enlisted to care for him. Their interest in the child never extended beyond asking the grandmother how her day with him went.

Mary, the grandmother, loved the child with full heart. If she rocked him in her arms five hours it never felt more than a paltry five minutes for her. She devoured him with her eyes. By his second birthday he had equaled in height and weight the other children his age. At age five and a half, photographs taken of his kindergarten class showed him to stand the tallest of all. One of the mothers of the kindergarten children who had learned Bruce's name, remembered him from the time she worked at the hospital managing the incubators. She found it near impossible to believe that this was the same preemie whose parents had turned their backs on him... whose mother couldn't bring herself even to touch him. Mary assured her that Bruce was that very child. In the ward at that time the doctors said that even if he survived he would never grow to a normal height. They spoke of psycho-social dwarfism.

Mary kept repeating her insistence that Bruce was born with God's blessings. She had never identified with her family's church, and had decided early on that those in their black garbs were all imposters. The profound heavenly revelations that demanded the faith of the congregations never bore a trace of substance. With regard to the emotional investments of the same members of that congregation in their religion, bingo had totally replaced the scriptures... bingo and yard sales.

Bruce had to be fitted with glasses when he was eleven years old. He had also given Mary reason to worry by the amount of sugar he would add to dishes that needed no sugar. He would add sugar even to his drinking water. The doctors explained to her that this anomaly may be linked to his history as a premature birth with the added complications of a dangerously low weight. At the same time the doctors were amazed to learn that Bruce did not appear to suffer the disturbing sensory integration issues that plagued most of those with similar histories. He did crave extreme physical experiences such as demanding that the swing be pushed harder, or for the spinning circular bench and rail to be spun faster. He particularly liked climbing on the furniture, and more than once he had called his grandmother to see him touching the ceiling. She would smile, shaking her head as though thoroughly puzzled as to how he had managed that climb. She would approach him, raise her arms, and with a shriek of delight he would drop into them. In her mind Bruce was God's favorite. He wouldn't let him fall. But he was getting heavier, and continuing to catch him this way, she knew, would soon have both of them on the floor.

Bruce was an average student, but he showed remarkable talent at public speaking, and with his excellent time on the 100 meter sprint he made the school track team. At the school's public speaking competition his subject had been "The Good Old Days", and with perfect timing he had the hall exploding in laughter almost from the start. It won him 1st prize.

Those had been great days but they didn't entirely carry through to his social life at university. At eighteen, and responding to the persistent advances of several girls, he found that he could not be stirred sexually however hard they had tried, and however determined they had been in their ambitions to arouse him. Bruce was soon understood to be impotent and it became the heady subject of gossip. He liked girls. He liked being with them. And he especially liked sniffing their perfumes and warm body smells. But there was never even the faintest suggestion of an erection. There had been the occasional discharge in his sleep after reaching sixteen, but never through an erection. Some had suggested that he was probably homosexual, but that had never been a lifestyle that attracted him, or had anything about it he could identify with.

Perhaps because of their suspicions in this regard, the track team, the coach in the main, related to him with an unfamiliar coolness and distance. He left them offering excuses about the weight of his studies. He eventually received his B.A. in Economics and Business Administration although he could identify with neither.

146

months, with the paperwork, lectures, interviews and training exercises behind him, he left for Mali.

Black Africa instantly appealed to him. He liked the colors, the people, how they moved, spoke, dressed and ate, but what he enjoyed most of all was the way they could smile with their eyes. In Mali he was stationed at a distance from Bamako, its capital and was taken to a large village community just outside Sikasso. Here he found himself, in part, responsible for managing the logistics in setting up a medical dispensary initiated by the local government with generous American funding. With a smattering of his high school French, but mostly with his hands, he was able to communicate comfortably with the people. They all spoke Bambara, and Bruce was determined to gain a practical, if only basic proficiency in the language.

With him was a local girl, Macina. Attached to this name was another that, try as he might, he could never get right. There was something of a whistle to it. With each effort Macina would double over with laughter. Sometimes she would have Bruce repeat her name with a member of her family present and that always promised tearful laughter for both. Bruce would join them.

Bruce and Macina worked closely together and they became increasingly close to each other. One late evening, almost without understanding what was drawing them to each other, they found themselves naked in bed. Macina liked to pat his face and set her forehead to his. Then, with an erection that could not have been stronger, Bruce made love to her. Macina seemed to perfectly understand, perhaps even anticipate Bruce's initial, uncertain and hesitant moves, and it had been her body that first found his. They became lovers with the marvelous intensity of their passion reaching increasing heights with each nightly union.

However the morning immediately following their first time together Bruce discovered that his eyeglasses, with their thick lenses, were no longer necessary... that his vision without them was quite perfect. Not long afterwards he found how much richer his food was tasting. The craving for sugar, which for so long he had forcibly repressed, was gone.

With increasing instances of terrorism in Mali, with one malicious bombing killing many in a hotel in central Sikasso, the American government decided to have the Peace Corps leave Mali. Bruce felt he could not have a life anywhere in the world that did not include Macina. The inexorable bureaucracy at the American embassy in Bamaco was horrific. A lesser determined person would have had his will thoroughly crushed, but seemingly with everything about to be lost ,by some surprising turn of fate they were legally wed at the embassy with Macina receiving the necessary travel documents.

William and Sandra never sought to disguise how remote they felt from Bruce. Nevertheless Christmas and Thanksgiving were two occasions when they would collect together in one place as family. When Bruce returned from Mali with this black as night woman as his legal wife they turned their backs on both. They never called Macina by her name but would refer to her the axe face. Her narrow and finely etched nose over equally narrow wedge shaped lips, with her thick braided hair at the back of her head probably served as the inspiration for their impoverished humanity and demeaning grossness.

Mary warned them that Bruce remained blessed by God and that it was a divine hand that had delivered Macina to their son. Mary would remind them of all the ailments he had suffered from birth that were destined to last a lifetime. Yet not a trace of any remained after Macina had been introduced into his life. They were not moved.

It happened one late night when returning from a holiday at Reno and nearby Lake Tahoe, William and Sandra landed at O'Hare airport, collected their car at the long term parking area, and started out on the thirty mile drive to their home. Somewhere along the way the engine had overheated and William pulled the car over to the shoulder loudly cursing the sudden inconvenience. A speeding semi-trailer had the car in its lights but it slammed into the vehicle instantly killing both William and Sandra.

As the sole heir Bruce inherited their fine home and considerable financial resources. It came to over ten million dollars. Macina insisted that Bruce not touch a single penny. Bruce was doing well in his own right, climbing rapidly to very near the position of a director in the branch of a large European bank. But Macina was adamant. She begged, cried and pleaded – even successfully enlisting his aging grandmother to try to convince him not to have anything to do with whatever had belonged to his parents.

Bruce could not understand her enormous emotional investment in having him turn his back on ten million dollars. When her efforts failed she packed a small suitcase, listened to no arguments that would have had her change her mind, and returned to Mali. She was pregnant with their son at the time, but this Bruce learned only a year later.

Not long after his inheritance reached his own bank accounts his vision began to fail, and he found himself again without a sense of taste. Mary had passed away very peacefully in her sleep, but with Macina's departure, it was clear that she too had distanced herself from him. The bank where he worked proved coldly unsympathetic to his increasing visual impairment and he was subsequently reduced in rank. It was expected that he would quit. It was about two months after Macina returned to Mali that Bruce learned that he was again sexually impotent and would likely remain so for the rest of his life.

30. A Bed of Roses

When his father passed away of a heart attack, Benjamin left university and returned to his small town and the lands in the English midlands, where, through four generations, his family had grown roses. It had always been roses, and the walls of his home had paintings and photographs of roses from the nursery's very first days. His grandfather had tried his hand with some notable successes at hybridizing new garden varieties, and the low greenhouses he built over seventy years ago, for that purpose were still there. The moss at the edges of the glass panes everywhere had their green and grey tint testified to the venerable age both of the greenhouses and the nursery itself. His father had also carried on with hybridizing programs with a few modest successes as well, and now everything was left to Benjamin to decide the nursery's future.

Benjamin had two older sisters, Veronica and Victoria, both married – none too happily – with Veronica in New Zealand and Victoria in Australia. Veronica and her considerably older, brutish, husband raised sheep on their lands outside of Christchurch, and Victoria, separated from her cocaine addicted husband, owned a hairdressing salon in Sydney.

Benjamin always knew that he would be returning to the nursery. He could remember how, as a thirteen year old, he had come upon the first April bloom of the Dutch rose, *Comtesse Vandal*, and thought that nothing in the world could be as beautiful, or as perfect, as this rose. It would happen on occasion when he would be in the company of a soft-voiced, exquisitely sculptured woman having the fairest porcelain complexion, that he would have a flash recall of the absolute perfection of that bloom with its delicate petals graced with its light porcelain pink and hint of copper tints.

His mother lived in their large eight room home along with her sister confined to a wheelchair. They got along marvelously well together and, truth be told, needed no one else in their lives. Apart from the meals at noon and afternoon tea, and at times when they went shopping in Lutterworth off the M1, or to a more daring outing at Rugby, they kept entirely to themselves and out of sight. Evening meals for the men, their numbers now reduced to only one, a mister Joe who managed all the nursery's operations, were invariably had at the nearby pub.

When Benjamin arrived at the nursery, and after his father's funeral (which had been sparsely attended largely because of the man's dark misogynistic attitudes and bitter feuds with the local council) Benjamin took careful study of the nursery's assets and liabilities. The multiflora rootstalks were all planted, but their cost set the nursery a tad in the red at the bank. However the three Dutch and two Irish lads who would be arriving in about a month's time with their practiced knives to do the budding, would weigh the coffers down with a far heavier expenditure. Nothing had changed in this regard in the last twenty years.

Benjamin had several meetings with the town council and did his best, behind a smile, to explain his father's old world stubborn single-mindedness. He succeeded in carving out a friendlier and more accommodating working relationship with them, and they did confess being aware that the good name of the nursery contributed to the good name of their small town. They were grateful as well for the visitors reaching them from far afield and who would leave some money behind with the few small shops along the main road.

Mister Joe had collected budwood from over two hundred varieties – hybrid teas, floribundas, sweethearts, polyanthas, grandifloras, miniatures, climbers and tree roses. There was also a collection of old classic roses, some quite rare, with a single hybrid perpetual, the heavily and heavenly scented *American Beauty.*

More labor reached the nursery when the roses were lifted from the ground sorted and stored. Orders started to be filled and the bank's loans were repaid in good time. Benjamin also had ideas about which varieties, if brought together, might produce new and commercially successful cultivars. He refilled the brick troughs with fresh peat moss, red-worm humus, and enriched the soil where the seedlings would (hopefully) take root and find first light.

In the months between May and October the rose fields delivered to the visitors a tapestry of colors in rows that seemingly had no end. It invariably distanced the people from the rush of the grey cities where they had their homes, and so often intoxicated their senses with something verging on the hypnotic.

That seemed to be the effect it had on one Mrs. Lydia Johnson who came to see the roses from a farm about five kilometers to the south. She made a large order and insisted that Benjamin visit her home personally to plan with her what to plant where. Benjamin suggested that the man who could best help her was Mister Joe, but the lady insisted.

Benjamin later learned that there was no Mr. Johnson and that Lydia Johnson lived with her nineteen year old daughter in a single story, stone house that, judging from the number of windows, had many rooms. The lawns and trees were impeccably sculptured and there was a long, wide T shaped area where the earth had been well turned over. To one side of the exposed earth was a wooden pergola, stained deep red against which a

Maréchal Niel climber was destined to grow. Inside the house with Benjamin sitting on a richly upholstered settee Mrs. Johnson set a cup of tea before him and joined him there with a cup for herself.

There was a minute or two of meaningless chatter when Mrs. Johnson suddenly lurched toward Benjamin and fixed her tongue in his mouth. She wasn't at all a bad looking woman, seemingly younger than how mid-forties finds many woman. Before Benjamin could decide how far to permit this scene to play out, her hand was inside his trousers. They continued in her bed. In fact they met again at her house three or four more times. This arrangement might have carried on for a while longer except for the intervention of June, Lydia Johnson's daughter.

June Johnson visited the nursery and introduced herself to Benjamin. Without mincing words and without paying any mind whether other people were in hearing distance, she said she knew about him and her mother, and that they always shared the partners they were having sex with. It was now her turn to be with him. *Her turn to be with him???* Benjamin studied the girl with pained and utter disbelief. But the first thought that came to his mind was that her mother was considerably more handsome than she was. He immediately rejected the offer and called Lydia to learn if she knew of her daughter's visit to the nursery. "Shared partners?" How many men, he wondered, had found themselves trapped in their web? Then again, perhaps "trapped was not the right word.

Lydia Johnson cancelled her order the next day. But a little over a month later Benjamin found June waiting for him on the fields. She assured him that her mother was outside their relationship now. Benjamin, however, would have nothing more to do with either of them.

All was quiet in this regard for about half a year. Then police visited him with questions about relations or other experiences he may have had with the daughter. It seemed that June had been slowly but systematically poisoning her mother with cyanide. This was discovered only when Lydia complained of being chronically short of breath, spent hours in bed suffering from a debilitating fatigue with her skin gradually turning a cherry red color.

During her trial June had a moment when she could share a word with Benjamin. "Did you know" she asked him, "that your father was fucking the both of us – for years… since I was fifteen?

31. My Taxi My Teacher

Martin (replacing "Muhammed" his name at birth) drove a Montreal cab not long after he emigrated to the city from Casablanca two years earlier. He had found a room on Saint Urbain, a street that had always welcomed immigrants and refugees since the turn of the last century. After the Jews had moved on to Outremont, Snowdon, and later to Cote-St. Luc, the street, particularly toward the downtown area, proved a magnet for the often neglected provincial French Canadian families extricating themselves from their rigid church centered lives. Their children now went to better schools and the girls stopped the popular practice of pulling all their teeth replacing them with false teeth. This practice, before the age of sixteen, had been their veritable coming-of-age ceremony. With time, however, the street attracted immigrants from Greece, the West Indies, French Africa, and the Middle East and their numbers now included Martin.

Martin learned early on to keep his opinions to himself. If his white Anglo-Saxon Protestant passengers (known familiarly as WASPS) were passionately against Bill 101 (a law obliging all public signs including shop names and everything on their windows to be in French), his French speaking passengers had the very same passionate investment in the passage of the bill. As a Muslim his Muslim passengers would sometimes ask if he didn't think the huge cross atop Mount Royal, around which the city was built, wasn't an affront to their faith. Was he or wasn't he for Pierre Elliot Trudeau? He liked the run to Mirabel Airport. When that closed to passenger traffic he switched to the nearer Dorval Airport although the bumper-to-bumper traffic cost him more in gas. In a word, Martin was comfortable here. He quickly adapted to the city and its people, and came to manage his life with relative success for a new immigrant.

His life centered around the wheel of his taxi. He invited twelve and fourteen hour shifts in his efforts to earn enough to return to Casablanca, marry the girl arranged by the families to be his betrothed, and return with her to a rented flat. But the road had bumps. There was the time he drove a stunningly beautiful woman from Dorval to the Ritz Carleton Hotel on Sherbrook St. On exiting she suggested demurely that if he would come up to her room – room 324 – he would get payment in full and more. "You're a handsome stud" she said with a soft smile. "It'll be fun. Remember, it's room three two four." Martin was stunned at the offer, and with his mind spinning like a roulette wheel, she took the small carry-on she had with her, and exited the cab. Closing the door behind her she told him to find a place to park for half an hour. In room 324 it was a heavy set man in an undershirt that had opened the door to him. Behind his shoulder, his wife kept asking what he wanted. Slowly it dawned on him that if she was coming to the hotel from the airport she had not yet been given a room. Describing her he asked at the reception if, only minutes ago, they could recall giving her a room. The clerk looked at him and replied icily in the negative. His eyes and the tone of his voice also carried the message that the Ritz Carlton was not a place for his kind.

Then there was the silver haired matronly lady carrying a full shopping bag and a small box neatly wrapped. After a long ride she asked him to stop for a moment in front of an arcade with several small shops. "I'll be back in just a minute" she said leaving the shopping bag and box behind. When more than ten minutes had passed Martin reached to the back seat and fetched the shopping bag. He found it stuffed with newspapers but was otherwise quite empty. Ditto with the neatly wrapped box.

Another time a young, primly dressed lady, possibly a schoolteacher, had paid him with two tens and received eight dollars in change. The bills were handed to a grocer who promptly picked up the phone and called the police. Martin had to wait for the police to arrive and then to be told that the bills were counterfeit. He had to pay the grocer a second time and then submit to lengthy questioning that included having his immigration papers reexamined.

After little more than a year Martin managed to save enough to return to Casablanca, marry, and return with his wife to a home he had rented on a nearby street. The reception he received was, in fact, the start of a hugely elaborate festival that was a tradition for Casablanca Muslims.

Five days before the ceremony was to start the bridal chamber was prepared. In the course of those five days the bride was given a bath in *hammam* – a sort of milk bath that promised to purify the bride's body. Then her *negaffa* which are older women serving as her attendants work to make her beautiful. They dressed her in a white *kaftan,* darkened her eyes with *kohl* and graced her neck and wrists with heavy jewelry. Following this her attendants conducted a *beberiska* ceremony where intricate designs were painted on her hands and feet with and earthy red henna. Finally they would sit with her and share with her the "secrets" a woman should know when she gets into bed with her husband.

Food was prepared in excess and the final ceremonies were underway. The bride was carried atop a platform and delivered to her husband who was also lifted on high. To the loud beating of drums and dances both were carried to the bridal chamber.

Muhammed was as caring, as considerate and as gentle as he could be. He well understood that his bride was shy, hesitant, and not a little frightened. He wouldn't rush to consummate the marriage. But the moment came when he penetrated her. He suffered her painful moans and sharp cries but something disturbed him. The same unsettling feeling he had had when taken in by those female passengers. He hadn't felt himself tearing anything. Then he felt her hand slip under his thighs as though arranging something with the sheet. He quickly rose off the bed looked at her hand in the light and saw it was bloodied. She had started shrieking hysterically. A small strip of leather that had been tucked under a ring had held a few drops of blood - either originating with a lamb or a chicken, but not with his bride.

Muhammed, again as Martin, returned alone to Montreal.

32. Only a Game

Sammy was the life of every party. He was a born comedian and the perfect extrovert. Along with his comic side he knew how to make a dollar. He made his fortune importing French, Italian and Chilean wines and Russian vodka. His imports from Russia included its finest caviar along with pickles and tomatoes marinated in vinegar thick with herbs in oversized jars. The secret, he used to say, was specializing. "Handle the best and stay with the best," he insisted, "and the world will line up at your door."

He was also very generously rewarded when asked to serve as the master of ceremonies at weddings. He shied away from bar-mitzvahs as his humor tended to be a tad racy and a throwback to the Catskill greats. Like the time he described at a very formal wedding, and to a very conservative crowd, his uncle Louie on the way to the toilet. "Y'gotta be 'specially careful with the people you bring into the house," he would say. "But our problem was that our uncle Louie LIVED with us full time." Here he would pause and let a malicious grin spread across his face. Then it came. "But always at least ten steps before reaching the toilet we'd hear the farts. They weren't just your ordinary, normal passing of gas farts. No. With Louie you were sure someone in the

house was revving up his 500cc Kawasaki motorcycle."
Appropriate sound effect followed for the benefit of a
lady or two wouldn't have any notion what a motorcycle
was.

There was worse. He would remind the young couple
that old age was also part of the package of living
together. He told the joke of the three old Jewish men
who hadn't seen each other in a very long time, so they
were into catching up… wanting to know how each was
managing.

The first one complained about getting up each morning
at seven and having an epic problem getting a few drops
out.

"I shake it and shake it and nothing… maybe a drop."

The second says. "That's nothing. Every morning at
eight I sit down, squeeze and squeeze, push and push,
and maybe if I'm lucky something the size of a pea will
drop out."

The third one sighs deeply and says "With me at seven I
have a wonderful Niagara Falls pee. Really wonderful.
At eight it comes out thick and heavy. So wonderful."

"So for God sakes, what kind of problem can
you possibly have?" They asked.

"The problem, "he said, "is that **I only get up at nine**."

For days afterward people would pass him on the street, show him a raised thumb and ask with a laugh: "Got up at nine again today, Sammy?"

On the street Sammy may have been the perfect extrovert. Not so at home. At home, with his wife and four children, the humor was gone and punishments were almost central to the lives they led. Every misdemeanor, however slight, came with a penalty. If it was his wife who came home from her shopping with something useless, he was not above venturing into the salon during her *Hadassah, Israel* meetings, in his underwear and asking innocently where she put the toilet paper, or why the goldfish were swimming upside down.

With his three older children anything from poor grades or sloppy clothes to sassy remarks to their mother always promised a reduced allowance. There were no if's, and's or but's. There were even subtle hints of punishment in the games he played with Rhonda, his four year old daughter, whom he loved with full, untempered, heart. Her happy giggle was truly as precious to him as the air he breathed.

Their favorite game was setting two soup bowls on the floor when sitting several yards away from them. They would bounce several bolo balls trying to get them to fall into their bowl. To get those balls Sammy had purchased ten bolo bats, cut the elastic, saved the balls and discarded the bats. It wasn't easy to get a ball to land in a bowl; those rubber balls, as small as they were, packed a lot of bounce. But Rhonda seemed to master the toss even better than Sammy. Sammy would complain loudly with every miss, and that would deliver Rhonda to hysterics of laughter.

It also meant that if Rhonda won, Sammy would get down on all fours, and pulling on his tie she would lead him around the room. When Sammy would win she would have to lie across his knees for a spanking. Both "punishments" delivered that rich, joyful laughter. To Sammy that laughter was worth gold. She loved the game, and she loved her father.

The years passed and Rhonda grew into a very beautiful woman. She carried herself with exceptional grace, and, with impressive grades in her studies, earned a Bachelor's degree in Political Science. She decided to carry on to a Master's degree and became increasingly involved with the Liberal party defining its local platform.

Sammy wasn't the happiest following her dating experiences, particularly when not all her suitors were Jewish. He couldn't bear the thought of her coming anywhere near an uncircumcised penis. But the day came when she introduced the man she would marry…

166

thank God, a Jewish boy from the Friedlander family of lawyers, in Westmount.

The Freidlanders were as pleased with their son's choice as Sammy was with his daughter's. The families got along extraordinarily well with each other, with each side virtually begging the other to permit them to cover wedding expenses.

The wedding was a gala affair. The caterer was brought in from a town in upstate New York. Sammy saw to it that the em cee he hired would not introduce so much as a hint of anything off-color. Altogether the ceremony, the meal, and the popular dance band, gave a perfect descriptive definition to the adjective "posh."

This was an idyllic time in the lives of all in both families. The couple honeymooned in Paris and returned to their own home in Westmount. After a very shaky and uncertain start to their sexual lives the couple eventually found their way. This happened when Rhonda succeeded in getting her very unwilling husband to take her over his knees and spank her hard whenever they wished to make love. Sometimes the spanking alone would bring her to orgasm. For Rhonda, when that happened, she felt she would be happiest if their lovemaking would end just there.

33. No Free Favors

Christopher had always been frail. As a child he was the thinnest, shortest and the smallest of all his kindergarten classmates. The clothes he wore always seemed to just hang on him. For this reason, and children being what they are, by fifth grade most everyone at school knew him as *"Chrishanger"*. This came in the wake of his class teacher who, one morning, commented on his rumpled shirt and trousers by suggesting that his mother put him in a washing machine, and fit him on a hanger. The children, plainly, had no monopoly on cruelty.

He had been the seventh of eight children, six boys and two girls, and at that low station he found his mother always concerned with those born before him and the sib after him. He would describe himself in later years as feeling like a neglected railway station, lost and forgotten in the night with the speeding trains never stopping there. For a split flashing second passengers might see a name on a post but a moment later the night would devour it and it might never have been there at all.

As a child Christopher liked collecting beetles, caterpillars, grasshoppers and just about anything that he would find hiding under rocks. He told anyone who would listen that when he grew up he would be a doctor.

He had found a discarded aquarium, filled it with a mix of black earth and sand, and had it colonized by ants. For months he kept the sides covered feeding them from the top with leaves and the grubs of insects that were always in abundance under the rocks next to the fence at the back of the house. Then came the day when he removed the covers and it truly was an amazing sight to behold. This had been his finest hour.

Not many fine hours were to follow. If he came into possession of anything anyone else may have wanted he would somehow lose it to them. He had this gadget with an eyepiece where if you turned a knob on the side pictures would appear to move on the screen inside. Others wanted to see it and it too was soon gone. Same with a regular sized football that got thrown around but never returned. There were cards of baseball players in gum packages that the boys saved and normally traded their doubles, but with only a very few traded back to him. So it was with a fountain pen he was given on his fourteenth birthday. Simply vanished. And it bothered no one when drinks had spilled on his new shirt at a class party. Through high school he was still called "Chrishanger", and he remained the frailest, thinnest, and shortest of all his classmates.

At university he studied accountancy. With his B.A. certificate he looked for work and found a position at a bank in the city's financial district. He had successfully navigated their interviews and tests, and before two years had passed he became assigned to their loan and mortgage offices. His work there became his life. He quickly ascended from a third level station to a responsible second station. By his fourth year he had been given signatory privileges and high level assignments in decision making. More than once he took a stand against decisions to award loans and mortgages, and more than once he opted for accommodating the requests. He had never been proven wrong. The bank's directors took note of the considerable losses he had spared them, and the healthy profits that might otherwise have been lost. More than what his learning had given him, Christopher claimed at a department conference, that he had a nose for people. No one had reason to think otherwise.

At noon one day, sitting in his favorite cubicle in the deli near the bank and eating from the dishes set before him, a woman suddenly dropped onto the seat across from him. She rushed an apology and hid her face behind the menu. From behind the menu she whispered that there was a man at the cash whom she didn't want to spot her. Christopher froze. He ignored his food, and tried to make some sense of what this odd woman, half facing the wall, was doing across from him. Nothing so impossibly strange ever happened to him before.

He guessed that she was in her mid-forties. Her sleeveless dress exposed sweaty armpits and stains midway to her stomach. Her dark hair was cut short on the sides and longer at the top. After a lengthy silent stretch she straightened up, put down the menu, smiled at Christopher and told him without a hint of hesitation: "If you buy me what you're having I'll let you see my tits."

Quite aware that any other man would have found her brazenness gross and insulting, instantly demanding that she disappear, Christopher, at the age twenty-eight and never having been with a woman, indeed never having ever seen a live woman naked, could only utter a weak OK. He felt himself having an erection. While she ate, largely ignoring her fork and knife, he asked her where what she promised could happen. She removed an eyebrow pencil from her bag, took his hand and wrote a phone number on the back of it. "Call me after seven. You're my man," It took two napkins to wipe off the grease she left on his hand.

At seven on the dot he called the number and it was her voice at the other end. At seven-thirty he was at her place – a one and a half room in the basement just off the garage. The address she gave him turned out to be less than a ten minute walk from his own place. He was glad for the chance to walk there and work off his nervousness.

He was standing in front of her when she took a step or two back, slid the top of her dress down to her waist and brought her breasts out from under the bra cups. When Christopher tried to touch them she stopped him.

"I said that you could see them. Nothing about touching them. Nothing is for free."

Christopher well understood the message. After another lunch at the same restaurant she had permitted him to touch her breasts. He ejaculated directly into his underwear. A few days later, after a dinner at a more upscale restaurant she showed herself completely naked to him and he promised that the next day they go shopping for a dress or two for her. That won him her educated hands where only his had ever been.

It was when he purchased a silver bracelet embedded with precious stones that she invited him into her bed. At this point he stopped and suggested that she come with him to his place. She lived in a pigsty. Everything was in disarray. There were clothes with towels, hats, underwear, coats and newspapers strewn everywhere. A rusting washing machine with a broken wheel stood next to the sink that had dishes still piled one over the other. He shuddered to think how filthy her bedsheet must be.

She agreed at once and very soon afterwards Christopher had his very first full adult sexual experience. Then standing in his bathtub they showered together soaping each other.

Her name was Regina – Gina for short – and to Christopher's dismay she let him know that her favors would always be commensurate with the gifts she received from him.

Nine months later Christopher was arrested for having embezzled close to six hundred thousand dollars through a number of fictitious accounts he had opened at the bank. When he gave the police a partial list of all that he had given Regina – a list that included four week-ends in London, two exquisite diamond necklaces, a dozen gold brooches embedded with emeralds and other precious stones, ivory and jade carvings, an expensive European car and a year's rent paid in advance at a flat far more luxurious than his own. She claimed she had not once in her life met Christopher or had ever been in his company. But they found most of what was on that list in her home in the drawers of a bureau. There was no safe. She was arrested as an accomplice.

Handcuffed and awaiting judgment in a court of law, Christopher knew in his heart that, given the chance, he would do it all over again.

34. Millie and Molly

Millie truly believed that she had been born under a lucky star. She started off sweeping the floor, rinsing the hair and generally preparing the women for the salon's hair stylist. She had left school before matriculating. With no money coming her way from her home, and no promise in her schoolbooks, she felt she had somehow to find a way to get solid ground under her feet. Her job in the salon was the first job offered to her and came on the first day she set out looking for employment.

She liked the work, she liked the people and the salon's ambiance. There was always happy chatter with the customers, and everyone came genuinely to like her. It wasn't long before she picked up professional techniques. She was often trusted to continue with the hair arrangements prior to the dying that the hair dresser had started. After a time Millie became practiced with the dying and soon showed a skilled hand with the fan.

A high point in her young life at the time came when a young woman, an off and on customer, asked specifically for Millie to do her hair – everything from start to finish. With some of the staff getting married, or leaving for whatever other reasons, Millie now had her own chair, and she did well. One morning a famous face showed up at the salon saying that her manager had made the appointment in another name. She said that Millie had been recommended to her and would she take her.

The woman was a popular young singer and Millie trembled frightfully within herself. Could this really be a famous, wealthy and popular singer, with a show of her own, finding herself in actual physical contact with her own fingers? Outwardly Millie displayed a mature and professional confidence, speaking infrequently, but understanding everything asked of her. The dying was muted and perfectly blended. The fan had never worked the sophisticated waves and flares of any client more expertly than in Millie's hand that morning. A week later the owner of the salon rushed in to embrace Millie. Excitedly she showed her a popular column on a daily newspaper's social page. There was a photograph of the singer showing off her hairdo, giving the name and address of the salon and not forgetting Millie.

Millie had appointments lined up for two and three weeks in advance. It was no secret that with such marvelous popularity she would be opening her own salon very soon. The owner advised her not to rush, that she would have her own salon, but to use the time she had now to learn more about costs, salaries, management, rental arrangements and whatever else that went into the economics of running a salon.

Millie never got that far. She was arrested not for possession of hard drugs but for channeling them to sellers on the street. Her ambitiousness had been without restraint. The ease with which she settled into her own furnished flat, no longer having to haggle over prices with shopkeepers, kept whetting her appetite for more. The drugs had promised a windfall of easy money. She had one persona during the day at the salon, and a very different persona in the late evenings with the importers.

Millie had no tools to accommodate this catastrophic reversal in her fortunes. She had had everything at the tips of her fingers and now it had all dissipated into nothing. A depression of pathological dimensions overtook her, and, for a short time, it had been necessary to move her to a chamber where she could not inflict serious damage to herself. Drugs helped her ease a way back to the structured routine of prison life, and she soon found herself again working as a hairdresser. Her moods improved when more and more of the women guards and supervisors asked her to do their hair. She became a favorite with all of them and learned about all the problems they were having at home and at work.

Millie shared a cell with Molly. Molly was a black woman, two years older than her, a few inches shorter but built like a pugilist. She had broad shoulders, a tight belly, thin at the waist and almost spindly legs. Molly was an aggressive type, forever threatening to dispose any number of the other prisoners with whom she had kept an accounting. Sometimes their infringements were as inane as making excessive eye contact, but most had to do with the bartering of cigarettes and soaps. Molly never knew her mother or father and grew up in a neglected orphanage until she turned her back to it before her twelfth birthday. She had made a life for herself on the streets. Without providing too many details Millie learned that Molly was incarcerated after having been convicted of manslaughter, and had twelve years to go before any possibility of release. The judge had Millie sent up for two years.

Millie and Molly became lovers. Molly initiated the physical intimacy between them. Milly accepted Molly into her bed and at first could relate to Molly as a man. Except for the actual penetration and having the penis in her mouth, every experience might have duplicated the experiences she had had with the few men who, in better days, had entered and subsequently exited her life.

Millie taught Mollie everything she knew about the new popular styles in false nails and nail painting. "It's become a big industry outside", she assured her. "If you know nails you can have a decent life wherever you go."

Molly was open to learning. Millie prepared a list of what to fetch. It took over a month, but the stock of false nails, files and paints eventually reached them. They arranged Millie's workplace to resemble a salon and to include a table and lamp for Molly as manicurist and nail expert.

Millie didn't love Molly in a manner limited to the experience of physical pleasures. Increasingly Molly became fixed in her heart. She loved the quiet and gentle embrace, the taste of her lips and the feel of her hand sliding through her hair. She loved the way Molly would hold her buttocks and spread them apart almost to hurting, and Molly's lips and tongue on her nipples and breasts felt almost as though they were an organic extension of her own body. She wanted Molly to own her body and would whisper this wish into her hair in a low, throaty voice.

After twenty months Millie was released. The news of her pending release devastated her. Leaving Molly, she felt, was like leaving with neither her body nor mind. Her few days outside the prison prior to her full release were mostly spent shopping for the few things she could bring back to Molly, and to call the people to whom Molly wished messages be delivered. The owner of the salon where she had worked was enthralled at the prospect of Millie returning. The fact that she had served time for a drug offence would add yet another attraction to her address, particularly with the younger customers who, for the most part, never seemed to have a problem with budgetary restraints.

The guards, the officers and the warden all wished her well, with many promising to visit her at the salon. The tears that flowed from her eyes were tears of grief, not joy. Molly had started keeping a distance from her, and the entire experience of her release felt as unnatural and almost as threatening as had been her initial entry into the prison. Outside the prison and back at the salon Millie functioned as though in a fog. Her business ambitions evaporated and she contributed little to the chatter around her. The image of Molly and their perfect togetherness overtook every other thought that might have demanded her attentions. After two months had passed Millie again met with her importer. From a payphone she dialed the national police number. Masking her voice as best she could she advised the voice at the other end that if they would raid the salon they would find Millie back with a supply of drugs.

Having violated her parole Millie was sentenced this time to be incarcerated for five years. Molly wasn't at all pleased to see her. She had bonded with a new lover who made it very clear to Millie that if she ever got near Molly, so much as touched her, she would slash her face with a razor.

35. Demons of the Night

Damon found his regular table at the corner coffee shop. He would come every Monday and Tuesday between eleven and eleven-thirty both mornings. Sometimes he would make an appearance on a Wednesday but that was rare and becoming rarer. Just as he would get his paper opened to the crossword puzzle his ristretto would be served in the thin glass espresso cup that he himself had purchased specifically for his short coffee. Sometimes a small cinnamon roll would accompany the coffee, sometimes a slice of toast with a pat of butter and jam. A cursory glance at the headlines invariably produced a grimace of disgust, but the better part of an hour would be spent struggling with the crossword puzzle in the New York Times, which, he was convinced, was what, in the main, had made the paper famous.

That morning he found his ristretto served to him not by the matronly woman who owned the shop, but by a young, heavily breasted, girl, probably in her early twenties, with straight jet-black hair falling almost to her waist. At this time, just as everything new that would be introduced into his life, now in its seventy-fifth year, would disturb him, so too was he certain that, delivered by this girl's uneducated hands, the ristretto wouldn't... couldn't... taste the same.

But it did. This had Damon study the girl more carefully to see what there might be about her that would still give him reason to complain. In this he was spared investing much effort because she had volunteered just about every detail about herself, and her life. Her name was Pia (which Damon instantly thought was short for Pee On Ya), she was twenty-three, and saw her future as a writer of popular romance fiction. Her parents had divorced when she was five and she was presently living with her father and his girlfriend. She had moved out of her mother's house because her boyfriend took to molesting her and exposing himself. He would say to her while unzipping his fly – even with her mother at the other end of the house – "This is what your mother is getting. Want to taste it?" The name "Pee On Ya" again surfaced in Damon's mind. She had just detached herself from a three month relationship with her boyfriend who was studying music because he had no imagination. "How could it be", she wondered aloud, "that a musician could be born without imagination?"

What had seriously disturbed Damon was that Pia proved wholly impervious to his requests that he be left undisturbed.

"I'm not disturbing you" she would say.

"But you are. With your stubborn questions you aren't letting me concentrate."

"You can concentrate at home. This is a people place. Don't you like me?"

"I don't know you, and you don't know me."

"I want to know you. You look different."

"Give me some peace please. Go to your other customers."

"OK. First tell me how old you are."

"Older than your grandfather."

"The one that's still alive. He's seventy-five."

"Same age. Now get away from my face."

Pia, however, was a persistent young girl and very sure of herself. Damon could not upset her however determined his efforts were trying. These efforts had included approaching the owner of the shop and threatened: "Either she goes, or I go." In the end he stayed and she stayed.

Sometimes when there were few customers and no one was asking for attention, she would sit in the chair just off his left arm. When Damon said curtly, after the first time, that he hadn't invited her, she replied, pouting, and promising that the next time she sat at his table she would wear a different perfume.

Over a period of several weeks she had him sharing information about himself that he himself could not believe his words were given voice. She learned that he was, indeed seventy-five, never married, lived alone, had seen serious action in the Korean War as a lad of seventeen, was awarded a Purple Heart less for bravery than for coming away with shrapnel embedded in his back and leg, and, until not too long ago, had been making documentary films on rural farm life that were screened nationally and that had received much acclaim.

She also learned that he came to the coffee shop only on Mondays and Tuesdays because those were the only days he might successful navigate the crossword puzzles. The other days he found too demanding. He found it annoying, if not a shameful testament to his gross ignorance (and encroaching senility) to be leaving behind large gaps of empty squares.

Damon lived on his army pension and what small income his documentaries continued to bring in. It was just enough to pay for a cleaning woman to tidy up the house once a week and to pay for his groceries, papers, beers and books. He was an avid reader of history books, his favorite being the tome Tuchman had written on "that son-of-a-bitch bastard" General Joe "Vinegar"

Stillwell in Burma and China. It had bothered him no end to be fighting the "Chinks" in Korea. He recalled the horrendous, murderous rampages of the Japanese in Nanking – the raping, the mad unrelenting slaughtering of women and children – that he would have preferred to be fighting again with them against the Japanese. All this he had shared with Pia.

When his cleaning lady fell ill Pia asked him how much he paid her. She said she could use well the money and he would be doing her a super great favor by letting her clean up his house.

Pia had been as good as her word. Quite apart from bringing the house into wonderful shape with fresh air adding life even to the wallpaper, she prepared a spaghetti bolognaise topped off with parmesan that could not have tasted better at a five star restaurant. After her fourth week she decided she needed to return at least twice a week. Damon had loudly resisted, never being able to understand why so young and energetic a girl would insist on being that close to one with so few years left to his life.

One day she arrived two hours later than she normally did. It had been raining ferociously and she had called earlier to say that electrical storms frightened her and she would miss that day. But an hour later she called.

There had been a break in the storm, and she said she was on her way.

With her work done the storm had returned and she asked to spend the night. Driving would be dangerous. At first he insisted that he would sleep on the sofa and she could have his bed. After rounds of argument and head shaking they both got into the bed. He warned her repeatedly that he was a very restless sleeper, but that had changed nothing for her. Although Damon had the lights out, enough of the moonlight came through the window for her to see his thin, hard, angular body with the bones of his arms and legs pressing against his skin. There could not have been an ounce of fat on his body. He slept in a tee shirt without underwear.

In bed she tried to embrace him but he pushed her hand away. He instantly rose to his feet forgetting that he was without underwear and said he would spend the night on the sofa. She pleaded with sincere heart that she only wished to turn from one side to the other. He returned to the bed.

At some time in the hours of that night he could hear the muted rush of the Chungchon waters to the west of his company. He could see Charlie Company on the crest of a hill just ahead of them. Their Patton tanks were firing without letup shaking the earth under them. Mongolian artillery fire rumbled in the pre-dawn sky. Mortars were exploding on all sides. The wounded were screaming. The roaring planes were raining down cluster after unforgiving cluster of napalm bombs on the Chinese hoards. Then he saw them. Shouting, screaming rushing down the hills toward them, bayonets fixed. He swung his own bayonet violently at those rushing him. Sometimes there were three and four. He tried shaking them off. There were loud, desperate, deafening screams. He could see their guts spill out where his bayonet sliced through their stomachs. He lunged, again and again. They were choking him.

Damon awoke in the early morning light and dressed quickly. Pia was still asleep. When she was still asleep after eight he thought he best wake her up. The storm was over and the sun was bright.

The ambulance carried her body out of the house. She had been pronounced dead. They suggested, pointing to the large, dark, red-purple-blue marks at her neck, that she had been strangled. With his hands behind his back, handcuffed, police delivered Damon to the station.

36. Having to Settle for Less

Myron was a bookkeeper. It had been his ambition to become a chartered public accountant but he failed the examinations, and failed them badly, four times. At forty-six had been doing the books for over eighteen years for a clothing retail chain with three shops in the city. At his job there was no station to which he might advance. Little was there to look forward to. Five years ago he was given a larger glass enclosed cubicle where he worked alone. This, he understood, would be the ceiling of his possibilities.

He was always having to settle for less than what he aimed for. He was a sub on his high school hockey team, and again a sub on the volleyball team. He was good at ping-pong but never made it to the team. It had been his ambition, once he got his B.Comm degree, to travel seriously to distant lands and perhaps come up with photographs that National Geographic might wish to publish. The farthest he got was to Costa Rica where he suffered stomach poisoning, returning home after spending three days at a hospital there. He was certain that it had been when he had been delivered by ambulance from his hotel to the emergency ward of the hospital, that his expensive camera and video equipment, tripods, lenses, light meters and all, were stolen. His

Spanish was poor, as was the English of the police, but the best they could do was to leave him with a record of his complaint. Never having insured his cameras, that paper was as useless to him as anything he would flush down a toilet.

Charlotte, his wife, was two months older than him but looked considerably older. She sold curtains, draperies and upholstering material at a downtown department store. They had one daughter who had pierced her ears so that each now carried six rings. He had learned from his wife that she had also pierced her nipples and some component of her genitals all of which now carried rings. Her tongue had been pierced as had the corners of both eyebrows. With his opinions – totally meaningless to anyone anywhere – Myron had settled for simply warning his daughter never to leave the house in a thunderstorm. "You're the perfect address for lightning" he told her. "And you're the perfect address for my ass" came back her reply.

Myron and Charlotte had long ago stopped having sex. Myron had been greatly put off by the heavy sac of fat dropping from her stomach over her pubic area, which also came to have bald patches. There were heavy sacs of fat dropping from her back and upper arms so that he found himself grateful that clothes would cover her body. He knew that there was nothing about himself he could brag about. The length of his body was a skeletal package of skin and bones. He still had all his hair, but heavy, black-framed spectacles, with thick lens merely added to his milquetoast persona.

With whatever concerned his bookkeeping Myron was as reliable as the sun coming up every morning. There had never been a misplaced dot, or an invoice overlooked. The banks trusted his calculations, and the petty cash, along with the cash that was supposed to be in the safe, was always there to the last penny.

There was, however, one facet of Myron's life that was a contradiction in every sense to the patterns that normally gave the definition to his life. About once or twice a year he would feel his mind and body being massively overtaken by impossible pressures that threatened to explode if not somehow given immediate release. Once, that release had come with bungee jumping. Another time it had been skydiving while strapped to the instructor. A third time it was white water rafting. But for the last five years he would take himself to Reno for long weekends. Gambling really did it for him.

He was particularly adept at blackjack. He could count which cards were out and which remained. Then he did the percentages. More than once he pulled a three to give him 21 – one over the combinations of kings, queens or jacks that the dealer later drew. Without fail, he would leave Reno with between two to four hundred dollars more than what he had started out with.

Myron's present weekend in Reno took a different turn. After an hour and a half at the table, and with some winnings in his pocket, he got up to stretch his legs. As he passed behind the players at the slots his eyes became riveted on what he would have sworn was the most beautiful woman he had ever seen in his life. It bothered him that she had a pail filled with quarters on her lap. It didn't seem that the two could possibly go together. Nothing would have struck him as being more incongruous. Those along the row were all faceless nondescripts. He couldn't take his eyes off her. The soft round curve of her backside, so snug in that tight yellow skirt, had him imagine how blessed was every man that had penetrated that backside. Myron went to the cash, changed a fifty for quarters, picked up a pail and waited until someone to her right or left vacated their stool.

What drew her attention to him was a pot of three hundred dollars accompanied by bells and whistles, that his third quarter had delivered.

"I wish I had that quarter" she told him almost ruefully.

"It's not the quarter" he replied without looking at her. "It's the timing."

"Timing???" She turned to face him.

"If you're not winning anything you probably got a tight machine." Myron half turned to face her while depositing another quarter. He knew better than to smile or make that he was in any interested in her as a woman.

"I got a tight machine???"

"Look honey, if you're coming up totally dry after forty quarters you got a tight machine. There are tight and loose machines. I think I got a loose one."

"You want to change machines with me?"

"Why?" Why if I got a loose one?" At the same time Myron got off his stool, motioned with his hand that she could have it. He showed no intention of taking the place she was vacating.

At her second quarter thirty dollars fell into the box.

"I think half of that is mine" said Myron to her back.

"It was my quarter."

"It was my machine."

After returning all of the thirty dollars to the slot machine she vacated the stool. Myron promised to tell her a lot more about the slots over steaks. She told him her name was Charlotte (NO!!! COULDN'T BE!!!) and that she was here with her husband. He told her that he'd known some Charlottes in his life. She took him on for a coffee. He explained to her the Law of Large Numbers, how some three wheelers were programed to give wins only with three cherries, and how these new computerized machines spin out thousands of combinations a second and everything depends on the lever being pulled at the right moment... that the combinations have been decided long before the wheels stop spinning. He explained the Law of Averages and the percentages guaranteed the house at the slots, the tables and roulette wheels. Myron was on a roll. With her eyes open wide on him and not missing a word he felt himself ever bolder and larger than life.

"Can I ask you something personal without you taking a swing at me?" He asked in the best macho voice he could muster.

"What?"

"Are you with the house or a player like me? I mean you look like a page from Playboy."

"With the house??? The house??? You mean a hooker???"

" Yeah. Sorry."

"You can have me for nothing. That answer enough for you?"

It went as smoothly as that for Myron. Nothing he might have planned would have worked out this way. If she had been available for a price he would have paid that price. Any price. He would have fixed the mafia's books for the chance to be with her. He asked about her husband and she told him that he would only come looking for her in a couple of hours. She would give him half an hour and only with a condom. They went to his room.

Myron was shaking almost uncontrollably. He poured himself a whiskey and some had splashed onto his hand. He looked at her and how she moved. Again he thought she was the most beautiful woman he had ever seen anywhere in his life. What, he thought, could she possibly be doing here in his room with him?

He was too nervous to undress just yet. He sat at the edge of the bed. She started to undress and showed him the most perfect sculptured breasts. Then she removed the rest of her clothes. Hanging between her legs was a seven inch penis.

37. You Can't Cheat the Calendar

Shmuel was the eldest of five children. When he was eight his father, a tall man, an intellectual with an imposing presence and the owner of a flourishing bookstore, had fallen victim to a debilitating degenerative disease of the muscles. Shmuel remembered that the doctor had called the disease by the name of an American baseball player. In the immediate wake of his illness his mother had collapsed both mentally and physically.

Shmuel assumed responsibility for the care and welfare of his younger siblings. On some days his aunt would make an appearance to help with the housework and prepare food meant to last a few days, but the onus of responsibility and the brunt of the work rested entirely on Shmuel's shoulders. It would be Shmuel who negotiated the transactions with the druggist, as not all the drugs were covered by the family's health care association. It would be Shmuel who saw to it that both his father and his mother took their prescribed medications exactly as the doctor had directed. He knew from watching his mother how to use the old washing machine, and he gave the shirts, blouses skirts and trousers out for ironing. Here too he had negotiated the prices delivering his mind with a stern and determined voice.

His two brothers and two sisters missed not one day at school. He permitted himself half days with the teachers giving him material to work with at home. If any of his siblings encountered problems at school he would intervene with their teachers. Every Friday he would clean the carpets and dust the furniture. The Sabbath table he prepared always had fresh *hallah* and he would bring his mother to the table to light the candles. He had his sisters say the blessings. He would purchase cleaned chickens from the butcher and with salt, chopped garlic and parsley, make a reasonably good chicken soup. He could prepare tuna salad, chopped egg sandwiches with slices of tomatoes. No one ever went hungry.

He was nearing his twelfth birthday when his father passed away. The end had come when the muscles of his lungs had given out. The family's health association and some government agencies provided for an African student and a Philippian woman to care for his needs in his last two years, but the anguish witnessing his father's horrific deterioration was impossible to bear for everyone. The children would cry in their sleep. Nightmares were frequent. His mother had become a day patient at a psychiatric hospital.

Perhaps anticipating the tragedy destined to overtake his family, Shmuel's father had taken out a life insurance policy. This was hardly more than a year before the amyotrophic lateral sclerosis, or as it was better known as *Lou Gehrig's disease* struck their home. Shmuel knew to be appreciative of the financial security this had afforded the family. There was just no way they could have subsisted on the paltry allowance the National Insurance would have provided. In his heart Shmuel knew this had spared him leaving school and finding work. He would not have thought twice about taking that step had circumstances demanded it.

Shmuel had matured well beyond his years. He saw to the preparation of his younger brothers for their reading of the portion of the torah at their bar-mitzvah rituals. It was a coming of age ceremony he had denied himself when he had turned thirteen. He attended to the car service that would bring his mother to the hospital and return her in the late afternoons. Through the years he had painters paint the house and repairs made to the ceilings where the plaster had fallen. He saw to wardrobes of his siblings and even to the hygienic needs of his maturing sisters. He was never shy about reaching the cashier at the drugstore with boxes of sanitary napkins. When a cashier once asked him why his mother didn't buy them herself, he left the packages in front of her, returned to the shelves, collected the same boxes a second time and paid at the drug counter. When he next visited the drugstore the woman couldn't find enough words of apology.

Shmuel got exceptionally high grades in his matriculation exams – enough to be awarded scholarships if he chose to continue to university. Because of the circumstances of his family he had to volunteer to be accepted into the army. He asked to join the air force and specifically for the program that would give him the wings of a fighter pilot. He navigated the very demanding course exceptionally well and it wasn't long afterwards that he proved the worth of himself, his instructors, and the school itself.

Before his twenty-fifth birthday it appeared that he found religion. By this time he was a ranking and active officer in the air force. He began to wear a black skullcap both in and out of uniform, and attend Saturday morning services. Those who knew him at first registered amusement, but that had changed to serious consternation when he took to wearing under his shirt the small religious cloth with the fringes at each corner. These fringes would protrude at his waist and fall over his pockets. He had regular meetings with heavily bearded rabbis and took to reciting in a muted voice many of the morning and evening prayers. The community of air force personnel who knew him, worked with him and flew with him could not fathom the radical and literally mind-boggling changes that had overtaken him. It was not without a measure of relief, tinged with an aching sadness, that they reacted to his announcement that he was leaving them. He tried assuring them that he was the same Shmuel they had always known. He convinced no one, and no one at the base had recognized him when he returned to visit there on Independence Day a month and a year later. Under a wide-brimmed black hat his face was now covered with a forest of a beard, long earlocks fell at both sides, and he was dressed in the black garb of the ultra-orthodox with the bottom of his trouser legs tucked into long black stockings.

Shmuel had identified with a particularly radical sect whose rabbi impressed his followers as having God's ear. Virtually every facet of his life had been dictated by this rabbi. He was assigned to a group practiced in enticing young people with an uncertain sense of Self to leave their secular lives and identify with this rabbi. The rabbi then decided that the time had come for Shmuel to marry and he arranged a marriage between him and a woman slightly older then himself who had converted from Catholicism. He was further instructed to have frequent sex with her when in her clean days. She was made partner to the same instructions.

When together in bed Shmuel would tell her to open her legs which she would do without uttering a word. He would penetrate her, deposit his sperm and return to his side of their bed. Everything would be conducted in absolute silence. The act was not for their pleasure but to accommodate the rabbi's explicit instructions. She would place a pillow under her backside to keep his sperm from spilling out. In four years she had delivered four children.

One of his sisters had taken it upon herself to update me on how his life was progressing. Because she persisted with her secular lifestyle – as did her other sister and two brothers – Shmuel, at the instructions of his rabbi, terminated all association with them which included not attending their weddings. We often spoke about the extreme adjustments his life had known. I tried to explain that every child needs a father to give it an identity – its place in the world – to bring meaning and direction to its life. The child needs to feel secure, with its well-being assured, by accepting without question the complete and utter authority of the father. "You can't cheat the calendar," I told her. A child isn't meant to assume heavy adult responsibilities. The years with all the enormous successes he had recorded, and with all the strengths he had demonstrated to keep the family functioning and bound together, cost him his childhood. With time, the vacuum in his life only grew more difficult to bear. A father wasn't there for him. A father wasn't there to give his life direction. He's there now.

38. The Life of a Moment

Wladek found the "restaurant" such as it was, behind the fenced gate near the end of the quay. It was a dark, bitterly cold night, and very late in the evening. A thick fog had rested heavily on the black, oily waters and he could feel the dampness at his neck. He turned up the collar of his heavy coat that continued to deliver coal dust to his nostrils. He cursed in silence. Turning the handle of the door he slowly opened it, then carefully closed it behind him. There was no one there. He made his way to a corner table unsure of what he would find. There he removed a small leather packet from one pocket and put it inside his coat. It held his passport and other papers. A single bulb hanging from the ceiling cast a kaleidoscope of yellow shadows over the heavy, wooden tables and chairs. Everything seemed to him as old and as tired as he was.

His ship had docked here two hours earlier. They had left in the night two weeks ago with a large cargo of lumber from the port of Poti in Georgia pushing slowly through the Black Sea currents to Novorossiysk. Here the lumber was replaced with tons of grain. With the grain came rats and roaches. It had always been this way. The creaking, ship, pitching and yawing in the churning waters, and the loud belching smoke stacks, had been his home, indeed his world, for over twenty years. It no longer mattered what they were carrying, from where or to where. Now the ship was sinking very low in the water carrying coal from Port Vera to Constanta. Here in Constanta the coal would be unloaded. Wladek had four days with many hours now to himself. He prayed for a bed, or a pallet on the floor. There was no returning to his cot on the ship. Layers of coal dust covered everything. It had lined his nostrils, his throat, and irritated his eyes. He knew he was too old and too tired to continue with this work, but he was alone in the world, the few people he once had in his life were all gone. He had nowhere to go.

He heard a door creak somewhere behind him. On the far side, pushing through it, he saw a tired, middle-aged woman in an apron hanging loosely from her neck. Her hair was collected into a bun at the back of her head. Almost against her will, shuffling heavy legs, she made her way to his table.

"So late in this fog. I should tell you there is nothing in the kitchen." She was Rumanian but spoke to him in Polish. Her voice was deep and throaty. "You're from the ship with the coal. I can see. Half of it you are carrying on your face. The other half is now on the floor.

"Przepraszam" (I'm sorry).

"All I have is a kettle on the stove."

"Looking down at the table, locking his gnarled hands together, he replied with a deep, heavy sigh, *"czarna... czarna kawa."*

She stepped away without reply and returned through the same door. A minute later she reappeared with a glass of thick, black coffee. Some of it had spilled on her fingers. *"Czarna kawa"*. With the coffee she brought the corner of a hard bread.

"Eat it. It will clean the soot from your teeth."

Wladek nodded his appreciation. She left him but only to cross to the other side of the diner where she sat herself down on a low chair and stretched her legs. She tried to better arrange the bun, and to collect the straggling hairs that had escaped it.

His first sips of the coffee seemed to warm his entire body. He rose from the table and walked to the front door. He felt there was somehow more life in his body now. "I'm not leaving", he said softly. "I want only to take my coat off outside... shake the coal off."

"Do you need help?"

Wladek could not recall a single incident in the last twenty or thirty years in his life when he was asked if he needed help. Not once. Perhaps not ever. He could feel his face suddenly flush with his swollen and knotted fingers beginning to tremble. He looked at the woman again before stepping outside. He thought of the matron in the orphanage which was his first home. He tried to remember if he had ever heard these words issue from her lips. Nothing came to mind.

Back at the table he asked her if she had a room that she could rent him for three nights.

"Nothing here" she replied.

They sat in silence. Wladek would bring the coffee to his lips just to wet them. Sometimes he would sip just enough to feel the brew on his tongue. His head was bent slightly over the glass with his eyes locked on it. His eyes, however, had lost their focus. The glass was a blur. His hands encircled it absorbing its warmth.

The woman hadn't moved from her chair, nor had she removed her eyes from him. The silence remained heavy. Suddenly they heard a hand trying the handle on the door. It opened. A tall man in a coat as heavy and as black as Wladek's let himself in. The men nodded to each other. He asked the woman if she had matches. She started to rise off her chair when Wladek produced a box from his pocket and offered it to him. When the man started to remove a match Wladek told him he could have the box. The man bent his head slightly, saluted his thanks, and left.

From where she sat she spoke to him. "My name is Adelina. People call me Alina."

"Hello Alina. It's a nice name. Thank you for this coffee."

"And how do they call you?"

"Wladek."

"Wladek?"

"Yes. Wladek."

"Listen Wladek, I can put some boxes down near the shed. With a mattress and some blankets. You can sleep on it if you like."

He thanked her saying he was grateful. Yes. He would sleep on the boxes. It would spare him, he said, having to breathe more of the coal dust into his lungs. And the boxes couldn't be worse than what he slept on in the ship.

Wladek had long ago finished his coffee. Adelina didn't come to collect the glass. They sat where they were, each with their thoughts submerged under the dense, amorphous, layers of their histories. The minutes might have stretched into hours. Finally she rose and motioned for Wladek to follow her. She led him through the kitchen to the passage where the restaurant's meagre supplies were kept. She found three heavy wooden crates there, turned them over and set them together. Then he watched as she prepared a thick pallet of quilts.

"Wladek" she instructed, "get out of your clothes. All your clothes. Everything you're wearing needs washing."

"That isn't necessary. You, the bed and the coffee is blessing enough for me."

"Just get out of your clothes. I'll give you what to wear until everything dries. I have overalls just your size."

Confused, not certain just where he was, what he was doing there, how he had gotten there, and who this woman was, he undressed completely. She had even pulled at his underwear when he hesitated. She gave him a long flannel shirt to sleep in. Then she pushed him farther along the passage and around a tiled corner where they came to a large washbasin and toilet. Next to the toilet was a shower. She dumped his clothes into the basin, pushed him under the shower and started the water.

"Don't expect warm water at this hour" she said, playing with the knobs at the ends of the pipes.

She handed him a thick bar of castile soap and a stone to rub his skin. But then she herself got undressed and joined him in the shower. She took the soap and stone from his hands, turned his back toward her, and worked the soap and stone with a heavy hand on his neck, shoulders and back. Some warm water started to come through the shower. Then she moved to his sides, dropped to her knees and worked on his legs, his toes and the soles of his feet.

Rising, she handed him back the soap and the stone. "The front you can manage on your own."

There was a fresh towel waiting for him when he left the shower. Adelina stayed behind. She undid the bun letting her hair fall to her shoulders, soaped her head and her body. Wladek could not guess her age – probably between fifty and sixty – but he would have sworn that the universe could not have produced a woman kinder and more beautiful.

The restaurant proved to be quite busy the next day filled with laborers from the port. She served them cold borsht, boiled potatoes, slices of ham, stews of horsemeat, fish in jellied aspic, black breads, with an assortment of whatever vegetables were available, along with tea and black coffee.

Wladek's second night started out on the same pallet but it was well into the night when Adelina brought him into her own bed. The bed was narrow but the night passed with each embracing the other. They shared not a single word.

On Wladek's third night with his ship scheduled to leave in the morning, they again slept in Adelina's bed. This time they held each other shifting their bodies with Wladek soon finding himself between her open legs. It had been close to thirty years since he had been with a woman this way. Adelina pulled him gently higher and he felt some part of himself inside her body. The union lasted only a brief moment, but for Wladek that moment was as rich and as full as what any lifetime might offer.

Adelina's face was awash with tears. She begged with full heart for Wladek to stay behind with her in Constanta. They could both run the restaurant. She had been living alone, and running the restaurant alone, ever since her husband ran out on her almost fifteen years earlier. He had left her this restaurant, and not much had changed in it since then. They could do so much with it together. Her license with the Port Authority was forever. They could have a comfortable life together. There was no one at all in her life. She had one sister who had emigrated to the United States and worked with her husband at a gasoline station in New Jersey. Her father was killed in the war. Her mother had remarried and left with her new husband to Australia. She had no idea where even to begin looking for her, certain, in any event, that was no longer in this world.

"Wladek" she pleaded, "you don't need that coal in your lungs. Let the ship leave without you."

In the morning the blasting horns of the ship announced its departure. Wladek had left the overalls, the long flannel shirt, and other the bits of apparel she had provided, on the same table he had sat at when he first stepped inside.

.

39. Strangers in the Night

In sixth grade at her public school Sybil would watch the other girls gushing with excited anticipation. The sixth graders, in all three classes at the school, had, churning in their minds, the dance party planned for the Saturday night just ahead of them. With few exceptions all the girls had dates. Sybil was one of the exceptions.

On the Thursday before the dance Sybil was asked to be the date of boy from her class. He was an inch or two shorter than her, with a cherubic face and with full cheeks painted with a permanent red flush. She knew that his call was coming as late as it was because no other girl wanted to be seen accompanying him, but she was grateful nonetheless.

At sixteen, never having had a date since that sixth grade party, Sybil would now hear the girls in her class talking about their "steadies". The difference between a "steady" and a boyfriend was that the former implied regular sex while the latter promised little more than a movie, a partner at a dance party, and long very personal talks over the cellphone. Sybil had neither.

Sybil would have had a "killer" body and men's eyes would surely have followed her, would her body not have been bereft of breasts. Not so much as a hint of anything was there to suggest that there was, in fact, a women behind the clothes she wore. Her chest was as flat as a boy's and a tad concave. She wore no lipstick, no makeup, no eyeliner, she cut her hair short, and preferred tee shirts, overalls, or a tight fitting shirt under pleated trousers held up with suspenders. When she was in grade school and early high school her body appeared awkward and without symmetry. Her hands seemed too long and her torso too narrow. But with the years a semblance of balance had evolved. There was no longer anything awkward about her body or gait.

Before graduating law school Sybil did serious research on the surgeons who undertook breast implants. Eventually she made her choice. She repressed her natural hesitation to represent herself to the world other than the way she really was, and submitted to the surgeon's educated knife. Before six months had passed there was nothing about her naked body that might have suggested that any knife had ever touched her. She had opted for the very thinnest film of silicone saying she wanted only the suggestion of a woman's breast and not the equivalent of a neon sign seen in the night from a distance of twenty miles.

She had opted for a law career. She had matriculated with particularly high marks in math, and had often been complimented when demonstrating an exceptionally fine eye for the details in numbers. She had been praised no less for her sure and natural grasp of the processes of calculation. She did well in English Literature, History, and Psychology, but found herself increasingly identifying with the refined mental and social disciplines that defined the practice of law. This was the world she wanted for herself.

Sybil started out with a generous six figure salary at a prestigious law firm. The company specialized in corporation contract and financing negotiations, comprehensive evaluations of a company's worth, and when called upon, with issues the government would have with state and municipal affairs. She felt like a fish in its natural waters and was soon co-opted into the company's most complex and demanding negotiations. A speed reader, she could go through a thousand pages of transcripts in a night and recall everything in detail the following day. Before her first year was over she had uncovered financial transgressions and inaccurate cost accounting figures, to a degree that made the company's clients appreciate they were getting their money's worth and more.

It was in her second year there when she met a young civil engineer on a seven hour flight to Zurich. Both were in the business section, she had had an aisle seat alongside his at the window. Talk between them started with the sharing of a newsmagazine. They both had two business days to spend in the city, and their relationship took root at that time. On her second night in the city Sybil vacated her room and moved into his in another hotel. They spent the first night together dining at the restaurant at his hotel. They were there again late on their second night but this time they shared one bed. Sybil had her very first true and complete sexual experience at this time. Her partner would not have suspected this as she had had her hymen perforated surgically a year earlier by her gynecologist. It had been at her gynecologist's suggestion, and now she was grateful for that. Undressing in his presence, exposing her nakedness to him, had excited her no end. In bed she followed his lead and their union went well. There had been no crescendo of clarions and no peal of church bells but she was happy it happened this way, in a distant city, in a comfortable if nondescript hotel room, and with a virtual stranger.

Back home he no longer remained a stranger. They married and brought a daughter into the world. Both were independently wealthy with Ron, her husband, making increasingly frequent trips to distant cities where his expertise at building bridges and tunnels was in much demand.

It was sometime during their fifth year together that Ron showed her a newspaper advertisement inviting married couples to join other young married couples to mutually experiment with intimacies at a private home. The cost to participate was one thousand two hundred dollars per couple and included a generous buffet with entertainment. A telephone number was given. Sybil instantly turned her back to the offer expressing her profound disgust. Ron said he only wanted to share with her what normally respectable newspapers were carrying those days.

Two months later Sybil and Ron agreed to have a go, come what may. The telephone number delivered a recorded message inviting serious responders to visit a downtown bar and to ask for the name given in the message. They were to appear as a couple for a comfortable get-to-know-you meeting with the owner of the home. At that timed both sides would decide if the evening might be to their liking.

The home was in an expensive suburb of the city and extravagantly furnished. The entertainment consisted of a young couple having sex in just about every imaginable configuration. Not all of it made comfortable viewing, especially when his tongue started teasing her anus, but this lasted only a few seconds. Both Ron and Sybil had turned their heads away to avoid that scene. So had others. But the two made a handsome couple and were rewarded with generous applause.

The evening was to proceed with each woman picking a number out of a bowl. Each was the number of a room on the second landing where they would wait for their male partner. The organizer of the evening knew which woman was in which room so that when the men picked out room numbers the bowl would not include the room where he would find his wife.

The man who hesitantly opened the door where Sybil was waiting was, in fact, the one she would have chosen had she been free to do so. She met him at the door and locked it behind them. They smiled at each other asking how the other was feeling. They embraced. Then they kissed with their lips only slightly parted and she could feel the tip of his tongue caressing her lips. They stayed that way for a long time. Sybil was feeling herself becoming very wet. She had melted into his arms having never once felt such excitement with Ron.

They undressed and soon found each other on the huge king-sized bed. Their lovemaking had no end. He kept telling Sybil how soft and sweet smelling her skin was… how wonderfully tight he felt inside her – that he had never been with a sixteen year old girl but that girl could not have excited him more than the gifts Sybil was sharing with him that moment. Sybil had never ever heard anyone say these things about her… that she could be so pleasing to a man. They repeatedly found the other's lips. Sybil wished to bury all of his body within her own. Overtaken with a crushing madness, her lips covered every part of him including there where she had averted her eyes with that couple. She told him she truly loved him. He replied in kind. He penetrated her several times. They could not stop kissing.

When they got into the car for the drive home there was some chatter between them but of no consequence. Ron had offered that his partner was "all right". They drove in silence, Sybil preferring not to listen to the radio. She knew, even when her lips had first met the lips of her partner, that from that moment Ron would forever remain a stranger to her.

40. Joel

Joel was a standup comedian. The thrust of his material underlined all the failures that had defined his life since he was born. It began with the fact that he had been born on the 29th of February so that by his thirty-third year he could count having had only eight legitimate birthdays. He once added up – give or take fifty dollars - how much he had lost in gifts, and presented his calculations to his parents. He had demanded a telescope for that sum. They bought him a comic book.

He was also a frequent visitor at the Atlantic City casinos. He was a fixture at the poker table without once ever coming away with winnings. There were times when he had missed his gigs having forgotten the time, the year or the century. The owner of the comedy club attached Shirley to him. She was one of two make-up room girls at the club, but soon challenged fate by becoming Joel's manager. She somehow succeeded to bring some semblance of order to his life.

That order, however, had a very short life span. Returning from the Atlantic City boardwalk to Manhattan in Shirley's '92 Pontiac, they were on the Atlantic City Expressway a couple of miles short of the Golden State Parkway. The car with, Joel at the wheel, side-swiped a cement truck and careened onto the barrier dividing the lanes. Then he swerved back into the swift moving traffic again striking the cement mixer which had tried desperately but unsuccessfully to get out of its way. This was a scene out of a slapstick comedy. The mixer lost its wheels and landed on two cars on its right side. The northbound traffic on the Atlantic City Expressway backed up for six miles behind the cement mixer. Joel and Shirley were ahead of the mixer and couldn't distance themselves from the scene fast enough.

Several miles along the Golden State Parkway Joel was stopped for speeding. The traffic cops were as surprised as Joel to find that the car could still do a hundred and twenty. But the couple soon found themselves arrested, not for the speeding but for being responsible for the accident which sent six people to the hospital, four of whom would probably have to spend the rest of their lives in wheelchairs.

Joel spent three weeks in jail. The judge had handed down a five hundred dollar fine for speeding which Joel couldn't come up with. He had argued that the Pontiac had hit the guardrail because the cement mixer, powering down the Parkway almost out of control, had sideswiped *him*. Not the other way around. The overworked judge let that one pass.

From there it was all downhill for Joel. His wife had visited him in jail, was unwilling to pay his bail, and wanted their car which, only then, she learned he had put up as an ante a few days earlier. With three of a kind, jacks, how could he lose? He lost. Shirley had driven him from the jail to his home. When he discovered that his wife had all the locks replaced he had Shirley call a locksmith to let him inside. The locksmith that showed up was a midget and Joel, somewhat taken aback at his size, asked him if he would be able to reach the keyhole. The midget made an abrupt about face, returned to his truck, and drove off. In desperation Joel stood atop an overturned milk crate that had been discarded, broke two windows from the side of the house, bent the frame that had separated them, and with great effort squeezed himself inside. He badly needed the toilet, but on his way there he found the house bare of every last piece of furniture. The phone had been torn off the wall. It fwas then he remembered that his cellphone had been without a service provider for the last two months.

Joel had about as many iou's out as dandelion puffs spreading in a wind. The comedy club he worked at had told him never to set a foot in the place again. He was in arrears at the bank with loans so long unpaid that they were surely marked off as lost. The seventeen dollars and some change that he still had in his pocket was the sum of all the finances available to him in the world. A dollar of that was spent for the bus that took him downtown.

He looked at the second and third story windows for a room-to-let sign. He found one, climbed the garbage strewn stairs in the dark, and found a floor that had the markings of a user's pad where the sick and destitute probably shared their needles. It was stifling inside. The roar of speeding fire engines made it impossible to hear what the woman who owned the place was telling him. He went, in spite of the noise, to open a window. With his first efforts the entire window suddenly broke away from the frame and crashed to the street. It had landed on, or very near, a panhandler standing against the wall. Joel raced madly down the slippery stairs to find the man covered in glass. An instant later the woman charged out shouting that Joel would have to pay for the damages. An ambulance chasing lawyer who followed the firetrucks had witnessed the commotion. He swerved to the curb, slammed on his brakes, rushed toward them and handed the panhandler and the woman his card. "It's my card. Take it. I saw everything. We can take this joker for everything." To the panhandler who was looking for his whiskey bottle under the debris he advised. "Go... now... just the way you are... now... to Emergency. Tell them it fell on your neck and that that you got headaches." Joel felt totally defeated.

Fired by a sudden desperate rush of adrenalin Joel fled the scene. He raced across the street dodging the cars racing in both directions, spied a narrow lane between two buildings and ran its length with whatever energy reserves that still remained in him. That lane led into a wider lane expressly for fuel tankers accessing the corner garages. He stopped to catch his breath when he saw a wooden chair minus one leg under the bottom extension of a fire escape. He knew why it was there – waiting for him.

Life was over for him. Joel could think of no reason to meet the hours left in the day. Slowly he undid his belt and fixed it to loop around his neck. He set the chair under the fire escape, balanced himself on its three legs, and started to knot the end of the belt to the bottom rung of the fire escape. Just as he started to check that his wallet with his ID was in his back pocket the chair collapsed, the knot unraveled and he fell heavily to the concrete. Nothing broke, but he stayed prone on the stone. He could move but had no reason to.

Suddenly he heard steps of people swiftly running up the lane in his direction. They were three men and a woman. As they passed, not so much as glancing in his direction, Joel asked in a shout what they were running to. "It's a fire. A big one," they shouted back. Joel collected himself and followed them. He remembered the noise of one fire engine after another rushing by.

The blaze was huge and so was the crowd that had collected there. There was a camera from a local TV station catching a woman shouting desperately that her three babies were still inside, but the firemen held her back. Joel made a mad dash for the building. The firemen tried stopping him with their hoses and that may have saved his life. He made his way into the inferno climbed up some stairs to where the flames were all around him. Then more stairs. Through the thick choking smoke he heard the weak meow of kittens not far from where he was standing. Inching toward the sounds he found three kittens huddled together in a box. He collected them, fitting them inside his wet shirt, and with the flames licking at him from every direction, tripping on cinders, he somehow found his way out. He found the crews of three stations with their cameras trained on him as he released the kittens.

"MY BABIES! MY BABIES! MY BABIES!" Screamed the woman hysterically as she raced toward Joel. Joel was now on the ground having suffered serious burns mostly to his legs. There was still smoke in his lungs. An ambulance with its siren wailing loudly raced him to a hospital. All that Joel could think of in that ambulance, behind the oxygen mask, was that, however hard he tried, he couldn't even succeed in killing himself. He was the king of the losers.

Overnight Joel became famous nationwide. For days on end TV stations repeatedly aired their footage of Joel breaking into the burning building, the hysterical woman screaming for her babies, and Joel crashing out of the building with the kittens coming out from behind his shirt. Stations across the country delivered the images to almost every screen in every home from the Atlantic to the Pacific. When Joel's senses returned to him he was frequently interviewed from his hospital bed. He told his sad story, hiding nothing, and never sparing himself the gross shame that seemed forever to be hanging over his head.

Money started reaching him from all over the country. His bank welcomed him with open arms and treated him like royalty. The woman with the kittens offered herself to him. She was not much older than him, but she lived alone and could give him a fine home with every comfort. Interviewed on one of the stations she was asked what those kittens were doing in the building. They were with the vet to get shots. The doctor himself had escaped with two dogs and a hamster but had forgotten her kittens. With nowhere else to go Joel had accepted her invitation. She was evidently very wealthy. He shared her bed that first night but for Joel it was like trying to make love with a rope. He left the next day, not only because of the failed sex, but because along with those three kittens were sixteen cats. With the money that was pouring in he covered his IOU's and other debts. He started up a relationship with Shirley and both thought enough money might yet come in for them to open their own comedy club. They would christen it "The Three Kittens Comedy Club."

41. Bricks and Bones

Sitting 21 rows deep in the massive auditorium, with probably another 21 filled rows behind him, Irwin wondered what the future might hold for him with so many new lawyers about to introduce themselves into a city already saturated with a populations of legal experts. He knew of the problems encountered by last year's graduating class and how many had been obliged to give up law for other professions. He wondered what other professions might await him if he found himself unable to find a place for himself in a law practice.

It was, nevertheless, an impressive ceremony and the reward for years of painstaking physical and mental effort. He would soon alight the stage, shake the dean's hand with his right hand and receive his diploma with his left. At that moment there would be the flash of a camera that would catch him for posterity in his impressive robes and white sash.

His doubts were not unwarranted. He searched the association's newspapers and bulletins, made endless calls, searched the newspapers for items on attorneys retiring. His most depressing hours would be when finding himself waiting for an interview in a room with a dozen lawyers, each having graduated along with him that same day.

In the end he decided to jump into deep waters and open his own office. He took to representing cases where the individual was without the wherewithal to pay for his defense. The city would pay him the absolute minimum for this service. It would be just as outlined in their manual for the hiring of attorneys to cover such instances. Even here he might be asked to offer representation services perhaps once a week. Rarely more than once.

In small advertisements he promised his expert service in the preparation of wills, property damage assessments, court representation in all matters, and accident insurance claims. It was the latter reference to accident insurance that brought Mr. Bill March to his small, street-level, one room office.

He learned the name but could not see much of the man. With his head heavily bandaged, an arm and a foot in plaster casts, the other foot thick with bandages, and probably with a cast around his chest under an oversized hockey sweater, Irwin started in to ask the man to have a seat. An instant later he saw that that would be impossible. In his condition he could either stand or lie, and the office did not have a bed. The man set one crutch against the wall, and approached Irwin at his desk, leaning with both hands on the other crutch.

Irwin ventured "You're here with regard to an accident?"

"Lucky guess" said Bill pausing for a moment to see if his humor got through to Irwin. "It's about my insurance claim that's too crazy even to describe. You'll get your percent from whatever you get for me."

"Normally there's a fee up front" said Irwin. "But let me hear whatever you have to tell me. Are you alright just standing?"

"No I'm not alright but I need a few minutes standing without moving before I can sit. A bench would be better for me but you don't have a bench.

The man was a laborer… a bricklayer most of the time. He had been working alone on a six story building and finished the job with a huge stack of bricks left behind. To get the bricks back to the ground he had filled a barrel with them using the pulleys at the side of the building to lower the barrel. Then he worked his way down the ladder that was adjacent to the lift.

He figured there had to be about 500 pounds of bricks in the barrel. When he released the rope from the concrete block that had secured the barrel, he didn't release his grip on the rope that was twice curved around his wrist. Weighing only 150 pounds he found himself suddenly jetting upward meeting the barrel at the 3rd

floor coming down. This explained the fractures of his skull and collarbone. But with the barrel plummeting to the ground he got carried to the top where three fingers, caught in the pulley, got mashed and broken.

When the barrel hit the ground with such massive force the bottom fell out, and now, weighing considerably more than the empty bottomless barrel, and still holding onto the rope for dear life, despite the damage to his fingers, he made a super rapid descent, again meeting the barrel at the 3rd floor. This explained the fractured ankles and the deep lacerations along the right side of his body. But worse was still to come. He fell onto the pile of bricks cracking ribs and three vertebrae.

"But God was with me and you can see I'm not in a wheelchair. My biggest problem now is I can't have sex."

Irwin wasn't sure it was his biggest problem, but he took the case. A lawyer's life, he thought, can have its perks.

42. The Artists

It was advertised as a week-long exhibition for artists
to show their work collectively, as part of the Spring
in Tel-Aviv Festival which included Hebrew book
publishers from around the country offering their stocks
at reduced prices. "*Shikeh*", as he was called – short for
Yehoshua – saw the ad and thought he might contribute
the two large collages he made to garner public reaction
to them. To describe them as unusual would be
gross understatement. One was a tall, dark, assembly of
six wide strips of wood, over broken glass, under barbed
wire suggesting a holocaust temper. The second
was supposed to be a representation of William
Blake's poem *The Garden of Love*.

> *I went to the Garden of Love,*
> *And saw what I never had seen:*
> *A Chapel was built in the midst,*
> *Where I used to play on the green.*
>
> *And the gates of this Chapel were shut,*
> *And Thou shalt not. writ over the door;*
> *So I turn'd to the Garden of Love,*
> *That so many sweet flowers bore.*
>
> *And I saw it was filled with graves,*
> *And tomb-stones where flowers should be:*

And Priests in black gowns, were walking their
* rounds,*
And binding with briars, my joys & desires.

The collage showed the steeple of a church, in wrought iron, with an inverted cross over the thick roots of a leafless tree, made with a mixture of sand, strips of cloth, wood chips and carpenter's plastic glue.

But on the Thursday preceding the opening of the exhibition all the contributors were called together with each given the number of the stall assigned to them. Shikeh hadn't considered that he would have a given space to cover when his two works were less than one quarter the stalls dimensions. He had the option of cancelling his participation. Instead, the following morning, he drove to a junk yard and collected large planks of wood, rope, tin cans, discarded clothes, and an assortment of whatever else he thought might prove useful. All this he delivered to his back yard. At the hardware store he bought nails, gallons of the same carpenter's plastic glue and an assortment of spray paints – mostly black, white, dark green and blazing red. Several hours later he had six "original" works in the process of drying.

Shikeh's wife refused to join him at the exhibition wishing to be spared the certain embarrassment he was inviting. But his stall had attracted crowds and he, in fact, had made his first sale that first day.

In the crowds was Emma, a Polish woman in her early thirties, and a painter of very intricate stylus and India ink drawings, who had her own stall not far from his. She was a dark beauty with pitch-black hair tucked in over and under her ears, piercing black eyes, dark eye shadow and no lipstick. Her husband, Yoav, looked after her stall most of the time. Emma thought Shikeh's works were different, but short of amazing. They might have been amazing, she offered, had he given the paint time to dry. And the one with a relief of a tree behind ropes was too weighed down by the gravel and sand in the plastic mix to hang on anything but a stone wall.

On the third day Shikeh's wife had joined him. A photo of his work with the crowds around his stall was prominently displayed in the newspapers. At week's end all Shikeh's works were sold save the two he wished originally to exhibit. The relief of a tree with the sand and gravel was purchased by the owner of an x-ray clinic. It boasted a stone wall. They became very friendly with Emma and Yoav who were also on a high of sorts having sold every last one of the many works she had displayed. When it was done they decided to celebrate with pizzas and wine, and were joined by Blanka and her husband, Dany. Blanka owned the Jaffa gallery that carried Emma's work.

The six had put away pizzas and wings along with 3 bottles of Italian wine. They all became quite drunk. In this state they reached Blanka's flat singing the emotive verses of the Russian and Spanish civil war songs. On an end piece under a lamp Blanka had Arthur Koestler's book on extra-sensory perception. Blanka drew their attention to the geometric figures Koestler had introduced, where readers might test their own mind-reading potential. Yes, yes, all six had become very willing volunteers to take the measure of their ESP. The figures were simple enough: a square, a circle, a triangle, a rectangle and a star. Blanka took a black felt-tip marking pen and copied the signs on index cards.

Each one in turn took a place against the far wall. The rest of us sitting on the sofa were to study one of the geometric figures, and, in our minds, transfer that image to the one across from us. Shikeh guessed zero out of ten efforts, Dany and Siv, Shikeh's wife, did no better, and Yoav marveled at his success guessing one correctly. Emma got a full ten out of ten, as did Blanka. They may have had a little too much to drink, but they clearly understood that there was something eerily unnatural here. They had Emma sit alone opposite Blanka with the cards, and then with Emma holding the cards. It was always ten out of ten. The moment the eyes of one fell on a card the other recognized the card.

Dany then suggested that one of the girls go through a short passage to a room at the far end of the house where there could be no possible eye contact between the girls. Each would be given a quantity of the index cards. Emma would sit with the four and make a quick sketch of whatever would come to mind.

She drew a shoe with a high heel, spectacles, a cup, a bug with six legs, an overhead light fixture, underwear, and a ring with a stone. Blanka would shout that Emma was doing the sketches faster than she could duplicate them... that Emma was the artist, not she. When the drawings were collected it was plain which had originated with Emma and which were Blanka's, but otherwise they were identical – other than the overhead light fixture which Emma had given a cylindrical shape with circles as a motif and Blanka had drawn everything circular. Both had the fixture hanging from a short stretch of wire.

The chemistry of that magical evening brought Emma and Blanka very close to each other. They would spend a part of every day together. They would laugh a lot and gossip about the inadequacies of their husbands. Without fail, each knew when the phone would ring if it was the other calling.

Each had suspected that they were leading themselves into a lesbian relationship. They would often kiss on the lips, if only briefly, and they were entirely comfortable feeling the other petting their breasts. They would embrace sometimes planting their lips on the neck of the other, and with a smile confess their love. At the same time they could not have been more different in the manner of their sexual expressions. Emma had her studio in a one and a half room flat at some distance from where she lived. She had had countless lovers in her studio with Yoav never the wiser. He would forever be enlisted to stay with their boy, now four years old, when she had "work" to do at the studio. In her heart Emma couldn't be sure the baby was his, suspecting it came from the seed of a boisterous Russian architect. She thought she would know for sure if the boy would grow in a way that suggested that man's generous height, angular jaws and powerful musculature. In any event, the paternity issue never concerned her.

Dany was Blanka's first and only lover. In her forties she was three years older than Emma and they had three grown children. What they did share, however, was their holocaust experiences with Blanka as a child at Dachau and Emma born in Auschwitz-Birkenau toward the end of the war. Emma and her mother had survived. Blanka had lost everyone.

Emma wished to experiment more with their sexuality. She told Blanka that it was something they had to do... that she felt they were like both sides of the same coin... that they were linked to each other organically. It would happen that one would have thoughts and the other would comment on them. This phenomenon had been repeated so often it no longer surprised them. Even the initial experience of amazement had faded.

They agreed to spend an afternoon in a hotel room. They first shared a shower with each bringing the soap to a lather on the other's body. Emma would bring the soap to the cheeks of Blanka's full posterior letting a finger rest for a moment on her tight sphincter. They embraced with the water splashing on their heads and cascading between them. Outside the shower each dried the other in the oversized hotel towels and both fell naked onto the bed.

Nothing happened. There was no passion, no lust, no heat and no urgency to the contact their bodies had made. They paused trying to fathom where exactly they were, and what exactly they were doing. They studied each other in silence, and suddenly, as one, they broke into a rich, high-pitched laughter. Again, as one, they reached for the pillows and swung them at each other. Then it was over and they embraced – almost as sisters.

Blanka said that for her sex with a woman was like trying to fit a foot into a shoe two sizes too small. Emma thought that the experience for her was fitting the foot into a shoe two sizes too large. But apart from that afternoon nothing between them had changed.

It was a hot summer day. Blanka was with Emma in Emma's kitchen trying to come up with a recipe for *halishkes* – cabbage leaves folded into a square over patties of mincemeat, rice, onions and whatever else, with each halishke marinated in a tomato sauce. Emma's mother was visiting at the time and took an instant liking to Blanka. The feeling was mutual. They couldn't agree how long it needed cooking but there were enough to test them when they thought they might be ready. When Blanka stretched out her arms in gloved hands to lift the pot out of the fire, Emma's mother asked Blanka about an inch long birthmark near her shoulder. It had her recall her first born – a girl with a similar marking in that spot – but who had long ago had perished.

"But she also had a much larger and much redder birthmark right at the bottom of her spine."

Emma, open mouthed with a hand searching for something to hold onto, mindlessly overturned a chair, and backed away into the table. Blanka tore off her blouse, tore off her undershirt, stepped out of her dress and turned her back to Emma's mother. There it was.

Blanka wasn't Blanka but Danuta. The Nazi's had caught her and her sister, Danuta's aunt, very soon after they invaded Poland. Both had been transported to Dachau. Her sister had instructed Danuta to call herself Blanka which could have been Czech or Polish. Danuta was from the Hebrew. Emma's mother had been caught in hiding later in the war. This was after the Nazis had shot her husband in the street. She had been transported to Auschwitz, duly tattooed, and there gave birth to Emma. What had made Emma's birth so significant was that the midwife was none other than *Stanislawa Leszczyńska*, the Polish Catholic who was with them and whom the church had made a saint for all the right reasons.

www.ingramcontent.com/pod-product-compliance
Lightning Source LLC
Chambersburg PA
CBHW071338280526
45787CB00001B/140